LOCAL HISTORY

David Iredale

Shire Publications Ltd.

CONTENTS

1. Introduction   3

2. Preliminary activity   4

3. Settlement of your neighbourhood   9

4. Some features of your locality   15

5. Houses   23

6. Industrial archaeology   26

7. Gentle introduction to documents   32

8. Maps   34

9. Estate papers   38

10. Town books   41

11. Church archives   45

12. Quarter sessions   50

13. Business records   53

14. Government records   55

Conclusion   60

Some record repositories in Britain   61

Index   64

1. INTRODUCTION

This book is for people wanting to discover, though not necessarily to write, local history. Every community has a history, and the history of every community without exception can be traced to some extent. If there are no written records at all, you have the evidence of the place-name; names of farms, streets, church; of coins and grave goods found locally; of the sticks and stones of village buildings themselves.

The local historian seeks to understand and to explain the origin, growth, periods of stability, decline and fall of a community that has had an identity and a life of its own. The community may well be older in origin than the English nation. Alternatively it might have been founded by the Saxons and destroyed by fifteenth-century wool-growers, greedy for land and for gain. It could be a Victorian creation.

The historian need not tell the whole story. He can choose his century and his specialisation: Elizabethan agriculture in Stratford. He can take a section of the populace: shoemakers of Newton. He may be unable to trace the community's origin and there may yet be no evidence of decay or fall. But he must use every source now available to ensure his history is interesting and worthwhile, to bring himself and listeners face to face with local people of past centuries, not as names and numbers but as earthy human beings. For local history is not a massive assembling of facts, but above all about men and women and how they altered the face of their country.

I myself have written a local study. I took the small corner of an ancient township where, in 1775, navvies dug a canal basin. I showed the origin, and growth until 1845, of a canal community of remarkable people who mean a lot to me now that I have, as it were, met some of them through their letters, legal disputes, wills and journals. In due course I learned to follow a set pattern in my research which I outline in this book. In short, begin by getting to know your locality as it is today. Seek visible remains from every century to re-create the place as it might have looked. Read widely. And learn how to consult archives as inestimably valuable sources of local history.

People are curious about old England, its markets, ports and villages, its bustling mill communities that turned our country into the workshop of the world, the centre of history's greatest empire. They ask about the making of the English landscape, that wonderful variety of natural and man-made scenes that delights or interests the eye. This curiosity it is the local historian's task to satisfy.

2. PRELIMINARY ACTIVITY

In order to avoid subsequent confusion, first clearly decide the scope of your study. Learning about Iron Age settlement in the area demands one approach, investigating industrial expansion after 1780 a vastly different one.

1. Define the bounds of your chosen area. Is this a civil or religious unit; or economic – Greater Manchester; or geographical – Amounderness?

2. In what period are you specialising? Not every place needs a history from 10,000 BC onwards. Middlesbrough is most interesting from 1830 to 1910; Silchester in Romano-British times.

3. Have you a special field of interest: economics, religion, genealogy, politics, archaeology? If so be careful you choose a town that gives you enough scope. The archaeologist would not really be the person to tell the story of Stoke-on-Trent, centre of modern pottery manufacture.

Research methods

In sketches, photographs and words fully record all sources of information. By this means you accumulate pages of notes on a single cottage, book or manuscript. Each set of notes should be consecutively numbered. Notes on a field survey might have the following kind of information.

Source note 27

Field survey at Blundell's Colliery, June 1967.
1. Precise location of structure (grid reference).
2. Name and general type (e.g. colliery engine-house).
3. Dates (e.g. built 1865, demolished 1965).
4. Purpose for which used (e.g. to house winding engine).
5. Short description of remains, exterior and interior, including machinery, building material, furnishings; drawings and photographs will be essential.
6. Details of relevant excavation and reports; reason for present investigation.
7. Name and address of site owner.

Next condense the information from all your notes on to small cards for a numerical index of sources. From notes on fieldwork all you need show on a card are numbers 1-4 above.

From notes on printed material write on the card the author's name, the title, place and date of publication and, finally, relevant subject matter:

4

E. M. Carus-Wilson *The Expansion of Exeter at the Close of the Middle Ages* (Exeter, 1963) – cloth exports 15th-16th C.; local cloth-producing centres; John Colshill, merchant – source note 214.

Notes on manuscripts receive much the same treatment:
1. Location of manuscript: Southampton Record Office.
2. Owner: Sholing Parish Council.
3. Document: parish meeting minutes 1894-8.
4. Subjects: civil parish affairs. (Source note 93.)

Your notes from reminiscences of local people must not be neglected. Give the informant's name and address and his subject:
Field Bank at Newbury, local legend connected with Alfred the Great. (Source note 47.)

All these cards will provide a handy means of reference to your source material. Try in addition to compile an alphabetical card-index of persons, places and subjects occurring in your notes. Have a separate card for each topic: corn-milling; Thomas Vernon, labourer; Iron Age fort; Brent Street. Record on the topic card all essential facts from your detailed notes of books, documents and surveys, referring by number to these source notes.

FARMING	
Strips in open field shown on air photo	(2)
124 acres wheat, 76 acres barley, 197 acres pasture, 200 acres wood in township, 1843	(57)
Ten farmers in village, 1716	(36)
Big Hey ruined farm, 13th C. – 1787	(124)
	Turn over

In the above example source note 124 records a field survey; note 57, details from the tithe apportionment at the parish church; 36, a printed poll list at the library; and 2, a photo by the Air Ministry held at the rural district council office.

Reading

Reading, perhaps through long winter nights, should continue during your intensive groundwork on the site. Use local history books, newspapers and directories to accumulate as much information as possible. Your local library might possess a good collection of local and national material. If you feel dissatisfied go to the central library of a big city like Manchester or to a university library like Cambridge. Better still, obtain a reader's ticket to work in the British Museum Reading Room for some weeks.

Begin with works on local history and archives in general. These must include W. G. Hoskins *Local History in England* (1959); H. P. R. Finberg *The Local Historian and his Theme* (1952), a classic pamphlet; F. G. Emmison *Archives and Local History* (1966); S. and B. Webb *English Local Government* in several volumes dealing with such matters as the manor and borough, highways, poor law, statutory authorities and the parish. John West *Village Records,* second edition (1966) is a readable, well illustrated guide for the local historian and teacher. Do not be too discouraged by – but try to read – R. B. Pugh *How to Write a Parish History* (1954).

Next look at the *English Local History Handlist* prepared for the Historical Association, naming useful books and pamphlets. The Standing Conference for Local History has published a number of guides to records. The journals *Local Historian* (since 1952) and *History* (since 1962) will yield information. In each issue of *History* the 'Short Guide to Records' should not be missed.

So you come to your own locality. Look for the *Victoria County History* for your shire and your county volumes of the *Royal Commission on Historical Monuments.* Sir Niklaus Pevsner *Buildings of England* series should be used with lists issued for each parish by the Ministry of Housing and Local Government on buildings of architectural or historic interest. Works specifically about your area might be seventeenth-century classics like Dugdale *The Antiquities of Warwickshire* or modern paperbacks like the twelve-part *Hatfield and its People* (1961-4). Arthur Young (1741-1820) in various *Tours* speaks of local farming practices, while other diarists marvel at industrial development.

Records in print

Many important documents are available now in printed form. It is usually easier to consult records that are printed rather than in manuscript partly because your local library can obtain books on loan where it cannot borrow manuscripts. Most books are supplied with indexes of place, subject and people. So always make sure your documents are not in print before proceeding further. Consult the library catalogue of the British

Museum or E. L. C. Mullins *Texts and Calendars* (1958).

The Record Commissioners published works like the *Valor Ecclesiasticus* of 1535, showing the wealth of English monasteries, dioceses, hospitals and parishes; *Taxatio Ecclesiastica* (taxation of Pope Nicholas IV on the English Church), 1291; and rolls and acts of Parliament. The Public Record Office issues calendars of charter, patent, close, fine, liberate rolls; calendars of state papers domestic, foreign and colonial; a catalogue of ancient deeds in the public records.

National societies publish documents of general interest. Thus the Harleian Society deals with heraldic visitations in Tudor and Stuart days; indexes of persons named in chancery cases 1385-1467; Anglican church registers like those of Canterbury Cathedral from 1564 to 1878 and of many London parishes from Tudor to modern times.

You will naturally consult your own local society. The book *Texts and Calendars* deals only with organisations that publish transcripts of documents or calendars of records. But many local societies prefer to publish articles on local history showing the fruits of research. Your area is bound to be mentioned somewhere in the hundreds of volumes already available.

Illustrations

Paintings, prints, drawings, engravings and photographs frequently help the local historian to gain a clear picture of his locality in times past. Johannes Kip (1653-1722) provided some splendid views of halls, parks and villages in later Stuart days. Did Samuel and Nathaniel Buck engrave a scene of your town, abbey or castle between 1720 and 1753? Your library may own published versions of these works. A collection of seaport illustrations relating to the whole country is at Greenwich National Maritime Museum. During the early nineteenth century the Bucklers drew hundreds of pictures of mansions, towns and church buildings. Many are in print. Others are in the British Museum.

The National Buildings Record in London holds illustrations of significant buildings and now deals with every type of historical structure under its title of National Monuments Record.

Air photographs

Photographs taken obliquely or vertically from the air are valuable aids to research. It is helpful to see your area in relation to the surrounding district or to study at a glance the entire village or town. Older photographs can show sites since destroyed by industry or housing. New photographs preserve a picture of your town as it is today before further development. Various marks in the soil and vegetation may reveal sites of

Roman villas, old field systems, villages, roads and industrial premises. Photographs taken obliquely, late in the afternoon, after dry weather and over cereal crops, produce best results. Air Ministry photographs taken vertically are excellent if read with a stereoscope. Pictures may be seen at some libraries or purchased at reasonable cost. The Air Ministry's collection has been taken over by the Ministry of Housing and Local Government. You may also find relevant pictures in the possession of Messrs Aerofilms or your local council planning department. It is also worth contacting the Curator in Aerial Photography, Sidgwick Avenue, Cambridge.

Newspapers

Newspapers and magazines may be found dating from the eighteenth century onwards. Numerous papers sprang up after the abolition of obnoxious duties in 1855-61. These documents, even when not mentioning your locality, give you a feeling for the times which is most important. You will read about crimes, riots, house sales, new buildings, tradesmen's advertisements, disposal of large estates, announcements of births, marriages and deaths, articles on local history and antiquities, political news and much else.

Nearly every big town supports one old newspaper or more. Some have survived independently, others were absorbed by rivals. Copies should be sought at newspaper offices, though some proprietors send files to libraries or record offices. Microfilms of papers like the *Manchester Guardian* and *The Times* are available all over the world. *The Times* published a *Handlist of English and Welsh Newspapers 1620-1920* in 1920 and this tells you what local papers are available.

Directories

From about 1780 printed directories provide excellent local guides to most places in the kingdom. After a history and general description of the district with details of post offices, churches, trades and gentry, there is usually a list of the more substantial inhabitants. Some directories list people alphabetically, giving occupations and addresses. Some put types of work in alphabetical order and place people in these categories. Take care to check information gained from directories because some contain legends, misprints and out-of-date statistics. But do not neglect this source which can provide information on your town's economy for a century or more.

Among the best directories are those by Baines, White, Pigot and Kelly, all nineteenth-century. Kelly bought the copyright of the *Post Office London Directory* in 1836 and his directories continue until the present day. Most directories after 1840 are very detailed, containing every fact you expect to find in a modern council handbook. For a complete list of national, county and town directories see C. W. F. Goss *The London Directories 1677-1855* (1932) and Jane E. Norton *Guide to the National and Provincial Directories of England and Wales, excluding London, published before 1856* (1950).

Museums

Visiting museums greatly helps the fieldworker. History and archaeology as well as science and industry are well illustrated in English museums. You can therefore see for yourself artifacts from the past like a Saxon dagger, an Elizabethan clock or a spinning jenny. Moreover the good museum sets objects in their proper context, reconstructing for you the society that made and used the tool or trinket. The development of industry, houses, ports, artistic life and much else is traced by skilfully created exhibits.

South Kensington Science Museum is one of the richest sources for technological and industrial history. There many early machines are preserved. The Victoria and Albert Museum shows period furniture, household goods and costume among its varied collection. The Castle Museum at York has a reconstructed Victorian street, corn-mill and prison. But nearly every town's museum can illuminate the researcher's path.

3. SETTLEMENT OF YOUR NEIGHBOURHOOD

So begins some important but time-consuming work on the site. This should never be neglected. Indeed, if you live in the district there is no excuse for not keeping your walking shoes handy, your eyes open and your notebook available the whole time.

First enjoy numerous walking trips around the district to learn where every stick and stone lies. Make notes of all you see. You do not need to be a historian to recognise that woodland lies to the west, a waterway to the south, a place of worship here, a big house there. Eventually you will notice the woodland consists of firs – a recent plantation; that the waterway is a canalised river; that the church is a chapel; the big house the manor-house. Notice exactly where village houses and streets lie in relation to hills, rivers, woods and cultivated fields.

It is important to point out whether the land is mountainous

9

or rolling plain, rich heavy soil or chalky upland, blessed with minerals, harbour or river. A relief model of the area or the Ordnance Survey map with contour lines will be essential for this work. Then find out the geological structure of rocks and soil from the various series of geological survey maps (especially the modern one-inch set) and from *Memoirs of the Geological Survey of Great Britain.* So now with the aid of maps, conversation with local farmers, reference books and personal walking visits construct a conducted tour of your area to whet your listeners' appetite for the historical explanation.

Every local historian should begin with this description of the lie of the land and face of the parish. Use words, photographs, drawings and maps to enhance your description of fields and woods; church and manor-house; homes, workshops and mills; wharves, ponds, rivers and bridges; guildhall, schools, gaol and playground. This first study might take years if you fully survey the community as it merits. Your resulting description can be the most interesting and valuable of all in showing to the knowledgeable historian why, for instance, few people settled your area prior to the Industrial Revolution. Your work may lead archaeologists to exclaim, 'Surely here is a perfect site for a New Stone Age settlement.' Never underestimate the importance of your daily walks and carefully recorded observations.

Why men settled in your locality

Now you will again have to look closely at your district, at all features, whether grassy mound on the high common, decaying stones of an old cotton mill, handsome town church or overgrown waterway. Your work at this stage is not merely descriptive but interrogative. What are these structures? What needs did they meet? Who built them? When? What changes of purpose have these places seen? So you come to the question behind all local history: by what stages have local people tamed the primeval marsh, heath and woodland?

Much of this work will require archaeological training and knowledge because so little history is in fact recorded in documents. Be very careful, however, because it is easy for the amateur to overlook significant remains through ignorance or, while excavating, to destroy without making proper records. In many ways it is better to call in an expert from your local museum if there is any digging or other disturbance necessary. He will in any case make a report for you, explaining the origin, growth and decay of the structure. Of course many sites like Stonehenge are already the subject of archaeological digs and reports. Read these reports and place the information in your history.

But 'archaeology' is perhaps the wrong word for our purpose, implying the systematic study of what lies buried beneath the ground. 'Fieldwork' is a better word, the study and description of men's still visible handiwork from the beginning until yesterday.

Your first fieldwork project seeks reasons why men founded the settlement in a certain place and not elsewhere. Remember that Britain is divided into two geographical zones whose pattern of settlement has been very different. The local historian in the lowland zone, country south and east of a line from Tees to Severn, will be dealing with pleasant rolling land of sandstone, gravel and chalk, not difficult to farm but open to invaders. Here lay compact villages surrounded by the open-field system of agriculture. In the remainder of the country settlement has been sparse, scattered and late. Rocks are old and hard, soil heavy, climate cold and wet, mountains bleak, forests thick.

Look for adequate drinking water, the basic and most important requirement of a community. Lack of springs or wells means no sanitation, washing or cooking and soon leads to disease. A town like Old Sarum, whose water supply peters out, ceases to expand. In some cases water may be piped from afar but this is expensive and rare. Water as a means of power or transport is also an important consideration.

Could virgin land easily be cleared? Was the natural terrain damp oak-ash or chalk beech; misty moorland or boggy heath; marsh or sterile thin-soiled furze? Would pioneers need the axe? Or could vegetation be burned? Or is the land such that only advanced tools and methods can make an impression?

Is the site sheltered from prevailing winds and storms? Could men create defences against flooding, wild animals, enemy invaders? The Saxons tended to found towns away from any rivers and Roman roads that enabled marauders to attack suddenly.

Find out from farmers and geologists whether the soil is fertile in its natural state. Is there sweet grass for animals? Can grain and vegetables, those staples of medieval diet, grow easily? What raw materials are available? Is there timber for building, fuel and fencing? Lime-pits and sand-pits, marl, salt, peat, walling-stone are essential for the provision of fuel, building materials and fertilisers. Where could fish be caught?

Then consider the site in a wider context. Men may have settled in the place with an eye more on the surrounding country than on the soil or raw materials of the town itself. Is the settlement in the heart of rich farmland, at the junction of ancient trade or military roads or by the most convenient river ford?

Did the town, lying between two differing economic regions, cater for the exchange of goods? Seaports especially come into this class connecting hinterland with other ports in Britain or abroad. Large numbers of market towns began life as informal open-air sites, usually at river crossings, where men met to trade.

During your extensive field trips contrive to bump into people who are able to provide clues about local affairs and history. These men and women often see the landscape with a new eye. 'If I were founding a village that's where I'd build, on the hill by the spring not down here in the marsh.' Investigate. Was the hill-top indeed the original village site?

Laying out the town

Why did men lay out your settlement in a particular way? What does the original plan tell about the lives of these pioneers? What features are to be sought? There are several excellent reference works on this subject including Joscelyne Finberg *Exploring Villages* (1958).

A typical community lies round an open space or green near which are grouped vital structures like the well. To the rear, houses look on to an encircling back lane. Sometimes this plan is defensive in origin, dating from early days of Saxon invasion, but the green may be just an animal stockade, the ring of houses and yards forming a wall.

The street village stretches along a main road, most often a busy trade route. Each house-owner wanted to face the traffic for commercial purposes. Sometimes the local land-owner may forbid building on the land behind the street, creating a street settlement of great length. A road leading to a bridge, monastery or castle may attract houses.

A village whose houses are scattered almost certainly results from individual squatting on common pasture or in woodland clearing at any date from the seventh century onwards. Some industrial places in Lancashire grew in this haphazard way during the years 1680-1820. But the dwellings are not isolated farmsteads, miles apart. They form a definite community connected by tracks.

Many settlements were not laid out according to a master-plan. Settlers added house to house as need arose. So meandering streets that still survive date from earliest Saxon times. Is there any rhyme or reason behind the meanderings? Why do lanes bend, seemingly inexplicably, or halt suddenly? What obstacles like castle, church, burial mounds, marshes, diverted these streets?

Town planning demands that one man or corporation own the whole site and possess sufficient wealth and foresight to carry through the project. There must be reasons for the planning of a new town: port facilities, market or fair centre, strategic situation, proximity to minerals or manufactures. The neat grid-iron pattern of streets usually indicates a new town either from 1066 to 1307 or from the modern industrial period.

Decay and desertion

Village sites and shapes alter to suit men's need. Houses that once were conveniently situated for farmers and traders may eventually be abandoned after enclosure of open fields, silting up of the river or opening of a new market. If a parish church stands alone away from your settlement you may find that the original village lay near the church. But why did families abandon their old homes and desert their village?

Look for traces of the two thousand deserted villages of England, destroyed to create royal forests and parks (from 1066), by Cistercian monks seeking solitude (1120-1200), by economic and climatic deterioration and by the Black Death (1310-1420) and by sheep farmers during the century 1450-1550. Study M. W. Beresford and J. G. Hurst *Deserted Medieval Villages* (1971) and the aerial survey by M. W. Beresford and J. K. S. St. Joseph *Medieval England* (1958). In the former book are county lists of lost villages known in 1968. Communities have been destroyed more recently by landowners' landscaping (1660-1790) or when local industries like lead and coal suffered reverses (1880-1960). Many rural settlements have been slowly decaying since 1850 because people have gone to towns and farms have been mechanised.

On the ground you should try to recognise deserted sites in parcels of rough pasture. The medieval house and croft site appears as a raised platform surrounded by sunken boundary ditch. Only in stone country can any house foundations be expected, as at Gainsthorpe in Lincolnshire. The town street, back lanes and tracks to fields and neighbouring villages show up on air photographs. The church, built in stone wherever possible, and the manor-house can be found without excavation. Old fishponds, mill-races, mounds and kilns also survive.

Boundaries

How old are the boundaries of your town? Can these be traced back to medieval or Saxon times? If so, why do they follow such and such a course? What present-day features like stream, round barrow, valley or ridgeway would be visible to the men of your Saxon community? Why do boundaries make curious

13

detours and zigzags? Can they have followed edges of fields that were already ploughed? Or do they take in a corn-mill or a detached field belonging to the manorial lord?

Markets

Some men deserted old villages when a market developed nearby. Markets were frequently held in churchyards (prior to 1285) before traders moved stalls on to a convenient piece of open country. Others doubtless took place on village greens or in main streets. Stalls were converted into permanent shops with dwellings attached, filling up the empty space, though there was resistance to such encroachments where the market was mainly for sheep and cattle. Building on the old market explains why in some towns two main streets, separated narrowly by shops, run parallel. In other towns a maze of alleys occupies the former open space. Can you trace the bounds of the original open green?

Suburbs

Distinguish the various suburbs created by expansion of the old town. An ancient town centre may include parish church, castle and market-place, though the two last-named often lie just outside town bounds. A second market, granted by charter on a different day from the first market, is founded in a new suburb. If you can date the various church buildings in a town you have an idea of the order in which new sections of the town were built. The building of houses and shops on every piece of land in the town centre is most noticeable during the periods 1160-1340, 1700-1890. Houses are given four or five storeys. Alleyways stretch back over former gardens.

Results

Fieldwork investigation will provide notes and sketches about all kinds of structures and implements. The local historian needs all these facts and more. But it is helpful for him to interpret the material for his reader. What light is thrown on society by these discoveries? What does the presence of a round barrow tell of man's life in the neighbourhood a couple of millennia ago? Fieldwork is only really worthwhile if as a result our picture of local man's development over the ages is the clearer. Fieldwork is about men and men's handiwork.

4. SOME FEATURES OF YOUR LOCALITY

Now it is time to investigate some features of your locality. The examples chosen below are the work of men's hands in different centuries. Some will defy definite explanation at present but your detailed record of what you see may lead future historians to an answer. Eric S. Wood *Field Guide to Archaeology* (1963) provides a concise description of many field antiquities from megalithic tombs to staddle-stones, as well as a section on the technical and legal aspects of archaeology. A very useful few pages are planned on the pattern 'if you see . . . it could be . . . '. Study also the Ordnance Survey's *Field Archaeology: Some Notes for Beginners*, fourth edition (1963). W. G. Hoskins in *Fieldwork in Local History* (1967) shows what can be achieved by the perceptive researcher.

Fields and enclosures

Early Stone Age people were nomadic hunters. But before 3000 BC the first farmers came to Britain. Stock-breeders and wheat-growers, they still used only flint tools and settled in high lightly wooded chalk areas like Wiltshire and the Cotswolds. There may be traces of stock enclosures or assembly places. Two or three concentric circles of banks and ditches are crossed by causeways. These camps are not hill-forts.

Invasions after 1900 BC brought an energetic people who introduced copper and then bronze and so settled in highland areas like Cornwall in search of tin and copper. These Bronze Age people traded and farmed. They built round cottages and farmhouses, the remains of which are seen in such areas as Yorkshire and Cornwall. With dry-stone walls backed by earth and pebbles, cottages are small one-roomed places associated with nearby rectangular enclosures for cattle-raising and crops.

Successive waves of invaders introduced iron in the sixth century BC. These people were farmers. Their fields are rectangular, possibly to allow for cross-ploughing. Air photographs reveal enclosed fields in areas like the chalk uplands that have never been intensively ploughed since the disruption of ancient society about AD 450. Cultivation terraces or lynchets may be noticed on sloping ground on the upper and lower sides of ancient fields that climb the hill. Boundary banks limit these fields on sides running uphill. Many lynchets date from later centuries: Anglian settlers in the highlands have left ploughing strips ranged in terraces along the dales. These follow contours and cross modern stone walls.

From the fourth century AD to the eleventh, invasions brought Anglo-Saxons and Norsemen to a Britain that was in the main still untouched wilderness. These new people preferred lowland farming and hitherto unsettled river valleys but pressure of population sent many into the hills. The former inhabitants survived in certain areas so that agricultural pursuits went on, possibly uninterrupted, from Iron Age to Middle Ages. Men pushed back the bounds of forests and heaths at first by a system of communal ploughing in open fields. They grew grain and vegetables. They kept sheep and cows.

Villagers created the open fields as they cleared forest or heath. Working alongside each other through much of the farming year to produce arable crops, they created intermingled unfenced strips of land. This is enclosure from the waste for arable, meadow and pasture. As such it is looked on as a sign of progress and well-being.

The peasant, in ploughing his strip or acre, had thrown soil towards the centre, eventually creating a high ridge. The strips vary in size according to lie of land and nature of soil. A bundle of several people's strips all running in the same direction made up a furlong. Wide green balks or occupation roads (best shown up by air photographs) give access to all the strips. Very many furlongs compose an open field, with a fence all round the outside but none round individual holdings. If you plot all the ridges and furrows or strips on a map you will gain an idea how the area of arable was slowly extended over the centuries, furlong by furlong.

Enclosure of open arable fields has continued from medieval times. Evidence of the revolution is traced by deserted villages; newly created parks and sheep runs; neatly hedged, privately owned fields, five to ten acres in extent. Look also for hedgerows of hawthorn full grown, stone walling, wooden fences and gates, ditches, field drains of brick. Enclosure from about 1730 created new roads with verges on both sides some fourteen feet wide bordered with trees and hedges. These run straight across country to new farms situated way out in the enclosures. Farm names follow the news. Around 1770 they will be Quebec, Belle Isle and New York. Old houses in the town centre became rows of workers' cottages especially in the period 1760-1850.

Tombs and temples

Neolithic (New Stone Age) tombs date from 3000 BC to 1900 BC. They are of earth, chalk rubble or pebbles depending on the district. The building material is heaped up to form a long cairn or barrow, flanked by a ditch, with the higher, broader end eastwards. Burial is by inhumation. Earthen long barrows survive in Wessex, Lincolnshire and Yorkshire. But more numerous are the stone-built long or round chambered barrows. Walled and roofed in stone with entrance and passageway, these megalithic (great stone) tombs have to be raised before burials take place but allow successive or collective burials over a period of time. Burial chambers, occupying the eastern end, have usually long since been plundered.

From about 2500 BC to 1500 BC men constructed sanctuaries like Stonehenge and Woodhenge possibly for ritual purposes in connection with burial mounds. An embankment with an interior ditch usually surrounds a setting of posts or stones. Such monuments are greatly embellished during the Bronze Age (after 1900 BC). Many isolated standing stones may date from this Neolithic period especially in the highland zone, indicating settlement in nearby dales.

Most common and noticeable of field monuments are what the Ordnance Survey calls tumuli – really Bronze Age earth or stone round barrows. They are most readily recognised in chalk or stone country where the plough has not been so destructive as in clay and sand regions. See P. Ashbee *The Bronze Age Round Barrow in Britain* (1960) for an account of some of the twenty thousand barrows in the country. Look for a mound shaped like an inverted bowl usually with a ditch and (possibly) surrounding bank. Round barrows date from 1800 BC to Saxon times. Their excavation, which may reveal a miniature 'house of the dead' ring of posts and rich grave goods, is the job of archaeologists. Beauty, symmetry and size of barrows with associated objects indicate a high level of civilisation and organisation.

Christian churches

Your parish church can yield many clues about local history. Its first foundation may be the result of missionary enterprise or of a small community's growing prosperity. A pre-Conquest church would be situated in an important centre – military, commercial or religious – perhaps in a pagan earthwork, near a holy well or a crossroads. Why was your church founded? Why on that site?

The beginnings of Christianity may be marked by a cross, antedating all religious buildings and set up on a holy or central site. Crosses are carved with symbols, designs and even words that enable an approximate dating to be given. It is therefore vital to seek traces of crosses, now built into church walls or used as stream bridges and gateposts, as evidence of early Christianity in your district. Celtic and Saxon crosses are richly decorated with carving. The medieval market or crossroads cross often stands on a pedestal. It is stone or timber and very plain. The site will be of special local significance.

Then complete a structural history of the church using any of the architectural guides like D. Yarwood's encyclopaedic *The Architecture of England* (1963). Probably an adequate study of the building already exists and this should be available at the library. Churches of nonconformists and Roman Catholics merit attention, but here you will probably not find a ready-made guide.

The font may well be the oldest object in church and village. Because the right to baptise was prized by early communities, parishioners carefully preserved the symbol of that right. Together with the parish cross this monument could be Celtic, Saxon, Norman. It may date from a significant year of local history. Are cross and font of local stone? Is the workmanship and style traceable in other local buildings?

The graveyard is worth surveying in detail mainly for its monumental inscriptions from Tudor times onwards. Inscriptions are usually informative about village names, dates of birth and death, possibly place of residence, profession and achievements, in most ways fuller than parish registers. Tablets, carvings and effigies inside the church may reveal biographies of local worthies, costume, armour, even humour. Medieval craftsmen loved to carve likenesses of villagers in stone and wood about the church.

Among the best-recorded and valuable of monuments are the brasses on floors and walls of churches. Because the material is latten, a brass-like metal, detail may be very fine. Portraits are regarded as quite accurate. Inscriptions are added too. For a full and classic account see Mill Stephenson *Monumental Brasses in the British Isles* (1926).

Fortifications

Iron Age defended sites, mainly hill-forts, are widely distributed. Some lie on rocky promontories or marsh-edges, and need walls on a couple of sides. But most stand on hill-tops, surrounded by one or more walls to enclose areas of from one to one hundred acres. In the lowland zone grass-covered banks and filled-up ditches with in-turned entrance may be visible, especially from the air. A stone wall and rock-hewn ditch formed the defences in the highlands, though stones nowadays are tumbled almost unrecognisably about the area. Few forts are earlier than 450 BC. Most of the strong ones date from after the Belgic invasion of around 75 BC. Cross-country stretches of bank and ditch were built not only for defence, but also as boundaries.

The Romans took Britain into the empire in AD 43. Towns, villas and roads were built. But the highland zone was never properly subdued and here are found many military camps. Consult the Ordnance Survey Map of Roman Britain (latest edition). Forts, permanent bases of legions and units, are rectangular with rounded corners and gates in each side. Stone walls are backed by earth ramparts and fronted by ditches. Important forts possess corner towers, a shrine and headquarters building of stone. Bank and ditch seem sufficient for marching camps. Traverses protect entrances to Roman fortifications.

The earliest Norman castles (1066-1154) have left only the earth motte or mound surrounded by a ditch and, possibly, an embanked enclosure called a bailey. There may be traces of the stockade and tower. Castles can be confused with barrows or windmill mounds if you do not look carefully for remains of the bailey, access road, well or spring, flat mound top and building fragments. Later stone castles are excellently documented in standard histories, partly because royal licences were necessary for fortifications. For any type of royal building (castles, gaols, bridges, monasteries) see H. M. Colvin *History of the King's Works* (1963-).

Moated homesteads and halls are very numerous. Usually built in the period 1220-1420 and abandoned by 1580, the rectangular sites may now lie in the midst of open country. Only the weed-ridden moat may be visible if the house was of timber. The moat served not only as defence against men and wild animals but as a source of fish. See F. V. Emery 'Moated settlements in England' in *Geography*, volume xlvii (1962).

Forts have been built to counter invasion threats by Philip of Spain (1588) or the two Napoleons (1802-70). Trenches, pits and mounds have frequently been constructed by the army. Do not label these remains as medieval castles or halls. Architectural follies and sham castles built in parks or on hills to please the eyes of Georgian or Victorian gentlemen should soon be identified for what they are.

Townsfolk constructed walls round their settlements whenever possible until late in medieval times. Walls protected homes, workshops and markets but also restricted spread of streets so that development took place on empty crofts in the town centre. In your investigation of walls try to decide if men were building on old, possibly Roman or Saxon, foundations. When did builders first extensively venture outside the defences? Why was this possible?

Roads

The history of every local track or road should be sought to reveal the economic development of your district. Pre-Roman trackways such as the Icknield Way on ridges of open country served as trade routes between river valleys or different economic regions. Roman roads are trade and military routes.

Major Roman roads are marked on the Ordnance map or mentioned in such works as I. D. Margary *Roman Roads in Britain* (1955-7). Roads do not generally follow ancient tracks because so many Roman centres were new towns. They therefore take straight courses across country, marked today by lines of major roads, parish boundaries, hedges and field paths. The Romans gave main roads good foundations, paving and side ditches which show up well on the ground even today.

But medieval ways are generally entirely local in purpose, going to fields, mill, meadows, church and pastures. A few led further afield. Look for green lanes built for some specific purpose like linking a village to its lord's court or a grange to a monastery. Salt ways and drove roads were not usually specially built for salters and cattle men. These people used ancient ways but through long usage gave their names to the tracks. Some roads may have led to a now deserted village or to strips in its open field. Old ways can often be discovered by noting the course of parish or county boundaries along hedgerows or paths.

Not many new main roads were laid down in England after Roman times until the present century. Medieval roads follow local trackways or Roman routes. Even roads built by turnpike trusts in the years 1730-1830 did not usually break fresh ground, save to cut out long detours, cross drained marshes and avoid steep gradients. Turnpike records are reasonably complete so you should not confuse new stretches of turnpike for more ancient main roads. Post-enclosure roads however tend to be bounded by ditches, grass verges, walls or hedges, whereas medieval tracks follow wide courses over open land, altering position as ruts become too deep and wet.

It is a good idea to plot the tracks of all roads with the help of contemporary maps. In John Ogilby's *Britannia* of 1675 (facsimile edition 1939) is an excellent survey of all main and cross roads then in use. John Cary and Daniel Paterson drew maps of roads during the great coaching era, 1780 to 1820. For a list of useful maps and guides see the somewhat outdated *The Road-books and Itineraries of Great Britain, 1570-1850* by H. G. Fordham (1924).

Forests and parks

Work out the chronology of local forest clearings. The latest enclosures will be small, irregularly shaped fields on the edge of high moor or low marsh. Look for names like Brackenthwaite, 'bracken clearing'. Men built dikes and ditches along the edge of drained fen, constructing roadways along these banks which still meander from hamlet to hamlet. Isolated barns and monastic granges (storehouses) may indicate comparatively late clearances.

But not all land was cleared. Royal forests were created as hunting preserves embracing wide areas of arable and pasture as well as woodland. Inhabitants were subject to harsh laws which may have retarded economic development. Consult Chancery and Exchequer records in the Public Record Office, London, for interminable medieval legal disputes and for detailed perambulations of great medieval forests from about 1230 to Victorian days.

Wealthy people enclosed wide areas for parks with hedge, bank and ditch, destroying communities if need be. A park is merely an enclosure where the lord kept deer for sport and meat. On this read E. Shirley *English Deer Parks* (1867). Usually created under royal licence the medieval park may enclose former waste heath or woodland at some distance from settled areas. But many parks founded in the centuries before the Black Death actually encroached on arable pasture and villages.

Pressure of population eased after 1350 and landowners extended parks without much difficulty. Tudor and Georgian squires and noblemen purchased these properties but finding the area too small or the view imperfect vastly altered the landscape. So they removed villages, planted avenues, dug lakes and erected sham ruins. Some parks still survive in one form or another, though others have been returned to farming use or sold as building land. In old parks may be seen fossilised features from centuries ago – like Roman road, deserted village or castle mound – that in ordinary circumstances would be ploughed out or built over.

A ha-ha is a low wall and ditch round the garden of a hall to prevent animals straying from park to garden. This type of boundary does not interrupt the view from the house. Ha-has have been built in many parks since Elizabethan times and ought not to be mistaken for castle mounds, moats or fortifications.

Place-names

Place-names in your area can provide much history if interpreted correctly. To look up meanings use Eilert Ekwall's *Concise Oxford Dictionary of English Place-Names,* fourth edition (1960); your county volumes by the English Place-Name Society; J. Wright *Dialect Dictionary.*

The settlement's name may embody the personal name of the founder or clues about topography in olden times. It can tell you to expect Roman occupation (the element *chester* means 'camp'); pre-Christian Saxon as at Weedon, the 'hill with heathen temple'; or tenth-century Vikings as at Wigston ('Viking's town'). The Newtons in Domesday are usually early eleventh-century in origin. But some places have been renamed by later invaders. Biddisham in Somerset is, according to its name, of Saxon foundation. Yet the earlier name has been preserved, Tarnuc, indicating Celtic occupation. The Normans sometimes added their own family names to older village names, creating combinations like Stoke Mandeville.

Evidence of pre-Saxon settlement in place-names is not uncommon. Many river names are Celtic. The British word *ecles* meaning 'church' in place-names like Eccleston generally shows a Celtic church on the site dating possibly from the third century. Some places called Walton were 'Welshmen's villages', evidence that a native settlement survived there when the English arrived. The element *stow* means 'a holy place, place of assembly' relating to the missionary days of Christianity. Many *church* elements date from a little later, say the seventh or eighth centuries.

Places prefixed by 'new' and 'old' have no definite date: Newbald in Yorkshire is mentioned as early as 963. But New Sarum is new in relation to Old Sarum, and you should investigate the reasons behind the founding of the new town. Why was Newport, the 'new market town', established? The process continued in Victorian days when new town centres grew up by railway junctions.

Street names tell of activity there in olden days: Bread Street, Goldsmith Street, Horsemilne Street (where the horse-powered mill stood). Names may preserve the memory of vanished features like town gates, crosses or walls.

Some names of villages, fields or lanes help in the reconstruction of the old landscape. The element *ey*, meaning 'island', seems strange related to an inland town. But at one time the settlement lay on a low hill within wastes of damp forest, bog or lake. A field with the element *hey* was once an enclosure out of the forest or heath. The name Sweden or Swithland denotes forest 'land cleared by burning' especially in the north. Numerous Woodhalls, Woodhouses, Newlands and Newhalls indicate the progress of post-1066 conquest of forests, forming 'hamlets in the wood'. Names can thus show if the land was once forest, waste or cultivated; type of crop or vegetation; ownership: 'churchflatt'. Lands once within medieval open fields may be traced from such elements as *shutte, acre, selion*.

Houses too tell a story. A farmhouse quite often takes the name of owner or occupier, and not a few names have remained unchanged since Napoleonic times, a golden age of farming. Tithe Barn Row may be cottages converted from a medieval barn where were stored church tithes like corn and vegetables. In Arkengarthdale ('the valley where Arnkel, a Norseman, had an enclosure') is a house called Booze. Some people would connect this with illicit whisky distilling in Bonnie Prince Charlie's time. But the dwelling is Bowehous in a 1473 manuscript, derived from the Old English and meaning 'the house in the curve' (of the dale or beck). Since the name is Saxon one can assume there has been occupation of the site since the eleventh century.

5. HOUSES

Now it is time to investigate the history of all local houses whether still inhabited or in ruins. To make the task more manageable why not choose only houses built prior to, say, 1860? The work is interesting for several reasons:

1. The community's standard of living is revealed in its homes: were Stuart houses in your area comfortable or not?
2. House building often implies population increase and economic growth; rebuilding of old places shows prosperity; ruins may mean depression.
3. Quality of workmanship can be related to specific craftsmen and families.
4. The order in which houses were built shows where and when the settlement grew.

Enjoy a session examining the more permanent features of the house. Draw a measured ground plan and elevation, make sketches and take photographs. If possible dissect the house to reveal its structure and building material. Try to write on your plans the function of each room.

Regional variations of style and building material make generalisations about the ordinary farmhouse and cottage unsafe. The size of the problem can be gathered from studying M. W. Barley *The English Farmhouse and Cottage* (1961). The author surveys in excellent detail the great period of English vernacular rebuilding from about 1575 to about 1720, taking the country region by region.

Certain points are stated with certainty. The lowland zone was, until 1750, economically more advanced than the re-

mainder of Britain so that houses there may, in style and comforts, be very superior. If two houses, one in Buckinghamshire,
the other in Lancashire, look alike the former may well date
from 1680, the latter from 1780. Northern industrial expansion
after 1750 reversed the roles.

It is impossible to overstress that many houses, especially
those with foundation and framework dating from before 1610,
are possibly a mixture of several rebuildings. Modern bricks
can shelter medieval beams. Who rebuilt? How was the money
and labour forthcoming? What significance do you attach to the
dates of reconstruction?

Remember too that most English houses date from after 1570.
There are exceptional areas. In East Anglia, for instance,
medieval prosperity of wool merchants allowed rebuilding
prior to 1520. Tudor prosperity reconstructed the lowland zone
between 1590 and 1640. The highland zone followed in 1660-
1720. Then northern England, London and South Wales were
largely again rebuilt in the period of industrial expansion, 1810-
1910. Victorians tended to copy older styles, so do not be misled.

For a detailed guide on how to trace the history of a house
with illustrations and reading list see David Iredale *Discovering
Your Old House* (Shire Publications, 1977). The following
paragraphs form merely a summary.

Ground plan and elevation

The single-storeyed cottage is typical of British dwellings
from medieval times till about 1780. At the centre lies the hall
or house, the common living-room that might also serve as
kitchen and bedroom. In the poorest houses – in 1320 and in
1720 – there is just this one room. The chimney might be a hole
in the roof, though frequently there is a brick or stone stack
situated in one wall.

Prosperous families built additional rooms on each side of the
hall: buttery (for ale) and pantry (for food) on the lower end;
cellar or storeroom at the upper end. Above the cellar is the
solar or best chamber, the master's private withdrawing place
and bedroom. The kitchen is often a detached building.

During the fifteenth century people of modest means added
a second or third room to their dwelling. On one side of the hall
lies the chamber or parlour. This serves for storing, entertaining
and sleeping and is always at ground level. The third room is the
pantry. Usually the family cooked in the hall because here is
located the only fireplace. The hall is still open to the roof but
side rooms may have bedrooms above, especially in towns and
wealthy country areas. This development is most commonly
found after about 1580.

Ground plans alter radically in the lowlands in 1575-1640, 1615–1700 in the highlands. Malthouse, milking shed and (upstairs) cornroom and cheese chamber are added. The house might get one or two wings and become shaped like an H, E or L. The hall may be open to the roof, though by 1600 owners preferred to insert chambers over the hall, lit perhaps by dormer windows. The wings are invariably two-storeyed.

In the south the chimney-stack is centrally placed at the axis of hall and wings so that both hall and parlour may have fireplaces back to back. Alternatively the fireplace backs on to the through passage so that the parlour then possesses its own stack. Highland homes often have stone stacks built like buttresses on the front wall near the main doorway.

Even the poorest homes often possess a separate sleeping chamber or parlour by 1650 and by 1700 a third room, the buttery. These rooms lengthways produce a rather long narrow dwelling suitable for the country but not for crowded towns. The hall is, however, still the centre of the house, the living-room and kitchen combined. Only after 1700 did the buttery turn into a kitchen and the parlour a sitting-room.

The square or double house becomes popular about 1680. With central staircase opposite the front door, this house balances parlour and drawing-room each side of the front entrance with kitchen and back parlour at the rear. The same hipped roof, sloping on all four sides and pierced with dormers, covers the whole house. Like many Georgian buildings the square house has an elegant symmetrical facade. The door, flanked by columns, is usually set between tall twelve-paned sash windows.

Terraced houses rarely date from before 1680. The earliest are in towns. London has its late seventeenth-century brick, two- or three-storeyed, single-fronted terraces, where each floor contains two rooms. There may be cellars, garrets, bay windows and protruding back kitchen. Space is gained by building backwards from the street. Country terraces of the eighteenth century consist of small houses, possibly with just one living-room and a pantry under the stairs that lead to the single bedroom. On these plans are based the majority of industrial dwellings prior to 1914. The most common type is the two up, two down dwelling with living-room and kitchen set one behind the other.

Not infrequently in the North speculators erected two rows of cottages back to back. Each house had just the one door and pantry under the stairs. These rows date from 1780-1840 and speak of pressure of population, greedy businessmen and local poverty. They are usually now converted into rows of two up, two down houses by penetrating the pantry wall and removing one staircase.

Regency houses (1795-1840) show traces of medieval Gothic influence. Builders introduced delicate iron tracery, pointed arches, verandahs, bay and bow windows. Symmetry is abandoned. Brick is plastered over to resemble stone. Country-like villas stretch down town streets. Victorians also loved Gothic details, trying to follow medieval or Tudor buildings. But their doors and windows are too large, their ceilings too high, for the historian to be deceived for one moment.

---

6. INDUSTRIAL ARCHAEOLOGY

Industrial archaeology is the science of seeking physical traces of the country's industrial past. The most important remains date from only the last two centuries but any discoveries may well have great significance on account of England's unique position as the first industrial society. Machinery in the local mill, for instance, might be the first of that type ever installed anywhere.

In order to recognise structures from all centuries gain an adequate picture of British industrial history. There is a short illustrated work on *Industry and Technology* (1963) by W. H. Chaloner and A. E. Musson. Sir J. Clapham and W. H. B. Court produced *A Concise Economic History of Britain* (1949, 1954). For industrial archaeology itself read R. A. Buchanan *Industrial Archaeology in Britain* (1972) and A. Raistrick *Industrial Archaeology* (1972) as well as articles in the journals *Industrial Archaeology, Transport History* and *Textile History*. Two series of works can also be recommended: Longman's *Industrial Archaeology* and David and Charles's *The Industrial Archaeology of the British Isles*.

As a start take photographs of your site using a twin-lens reflex camera to produce black and white pictures suitable for enlargement. An exposure meter, tripod and flash equipment will be useful. Record the main elevation of the structure to reveal features not immediately apparent like blocked-up windows. Next go indoors to take pictures of construction and machines. Notice especially types of building material, methods of supporting walls and roof, changes in wall alignment, rooms seemingly converted to new uses. Manufacturers' nameplates may help you to identify date and purpose of machines.

Modernisation has at various dates altered the shape of

factories. A large Victorian engine-room may now be the staff cloakroom. It is difficult, but not impossible, to recreate an original factory plan. Do not neglect cellars, attics and waste heaps. You may come upon scrapped machines not mentioned in company records but obviously at one time employed.

It is helpful to show an approximate scale by asking someone to stand in the picture or by using a rod painted at one-foot intervals in red, white and black.

Techniques

The surveying of sites and measuring of structures or machines demand common sense and a knowledge of simple geometry. The clearest introduction to this aspect of the industrial archaeologist's job is in J. P. M. Pannell *The Techniques of Industrial Archaeology* (1966).

In order to survey a site, equipment need consist only of a chain and measuring rod. But it is advantageous to have at hand the following:

1. A surveyor's chain (66 or 100 feet long).
2. Linen measuring tapes.
3. Markers (arrows, rods and pegs to mark points in the survey).
4. White plastic scales, reinforced with metal, divided into one-twentieth of an inch parts.
5. Field book with waterproof pages, strong cover, pencil pocket.
6. Drawing board and good quality cartridge paper.

The surveyor usually divides his area into triangles whose edges and angles he measures and records. His pencil sketches are converted into permanent surveys with a draughtsman's pen and black drawing ink.

Machines and structures may seem to present problems. But the most complicated object is made up of small parts shaped like cubes, cones, circles and so on. One difficult job is to imagine the form of all component parts, to draw each unit and put the whole drawing together accurately. You will need certain tools for this:

7. One sliding square with graduated blade and a spirit-level in the stock. This serves as a depth and height gauge and as a plumb rule.
8. Mahogany tee-square and transparent plastic set-square.
9. Steel strip tape (six feet) of the self-supporting type and a twelve-inch steel rule.
10. Outside and inside spring calipers for measuring diameters.
11. Bevel gauge and protractor to measure angles.

12. Plumb bob for finding the vertical.
13. French curve.
14. Square-paper sketch pad.
15. Compasses, dividers, sliding or pump centre pen bows.

If you have to draw machines for yourself begin by sketching important details – this is easier whenever an owner allows his machine to be taken apart – and then go on to measure the complete machine. Look for suitable horizontal and vertical reference planes from which all measurements may be taken.

Buildings, too, present problems to the unwary. Never assume that walls are vertical, floors horizontal and rooms square. Should you find walls supported by tie-rods, expect some bulging. Walls may be of varying thickness in different parts of a building. Windows and doors are often added or blocked up in the course of time.

The survey of any industrial monument should include the information mentioned already in the section on research methods. Ensure that your summary is so good that if the site is wiped out future historians will still be able to reconstruct it in their minds. Fill in the standard record cards issued by the Council for British Archaeology, London, and send a copy to the National Record of Industrial Monuments, Centre for the Study of the History of Technology, Bath University.

Power

By the side of streams search for traces of watermills that once were employed in grinding corn or producing textiles. Hundreds of fulling mills had migrated into the countryside to seek water power by Elizabethan times. Water-driven machinery introduced in the eighteenth century demanded improvement in the design of water-wheels, and cast-iron gears and wheelshafts are put to work. In districts where streams were not fast-flowing the windmill has been used since Norman days. The historian therefore seeks the site of mills, identifies their type and from records discovers the kind of work carried out.

The atmospheric single-acting beam pumping engine using steam power was put to work in 1712 by Thomas Newcomen to raise flood water from mines. James Watt's separate condensing steam engine of 1769, providing more power with less fuel, enabled manufacturers seriously to consider installing this type of equipment in place of water or wind power. In 1781 Watt patented his sun and planet rotary machine which was directly of use in driving factory machinery. The next year he devised a system of movable rods known as parallel motion to make his engine double-acting, applying pressure above and below the piston to double the power without increasing the cylinder size.

The earliest type of steam engine employed only for pumping or winding usually lay in a tall and narrow stone or brick building. The boiler is directly under the cylinder. A chimney forms part of one wall and the large beam protrudes through another wall, strongly constructed, to connect with pumping gear. Later boilers of wagon-type are separated from the engine and stand in low, domed and chimneyed buildings adjoining the engine-house. Beams of these engines can be entirely within the engine-house. Rope or leather belts transmit power to machines in the factory. Because such machinery was working throughout the nineteenth century, many traces can still be discovered.

Textiles

The textile industry – at first mainly wool – developed in medieval times, financed by wealthy families and organised on the domestic system. Look for houses of merchants and workers in country areas of Yorkshire, the Cotswolds, Wiltshire and East Anglia. In Yorkshire, for instance, note the tell-tale long windows of the upper storey designed to throw plenty of light on the looms at work. Many outworkers' houses in the Cotswolds date from 1750-1820. Textiles remained a village industry during this period of water-power.

Manufacturers next tried to concentrate textile workers under one roof so that all processes of making woollen, silk or cotton goods might be completed under close supervision. The Lombes' silk mill at Derby dating from 1718-22 is one of the earliest English factories. It had five storeys, water-powered machinery, continuous production and specialised functions for the workers. Not all factories were as big, especially those set up in converted corn or fulling mills.

Your task is to locate these early factories, then explain why the site was chosen and describe the power used. Search in the remotest areas like the Pennines, wherever water supply might be adequate. Textile machinery can be discovered and recorded. The spinning wheel and weaver's handloom, once common objects in farms and cottages, are now dumped in corners of sheds. Fulling stocks are the oldest power-driven textile machines, introduced in the twelfth century. Water power rotates a wheel which works hammers. These fall on cloth lying in a trough of water and fuller's earth, thereby cleansing and shrinking the cloth. The basic design remained the same even in Victorian days. Arkwright's water-frame, Hargreaves's spinning jenny, and Crompton's mule helped to mechanise spinning. Cartwright's powered loom for weaving (1785) did not prove economically or technically so acceptable, and

29

survived beyond 1850.

Mining and metals

By 1400 coal was being dug in many regions: the Forest of Dean, the Midlands, Durham, Newcastle. The industry expanded wherever men found easy access to the sea or to a large town. Spectacular growth came after 1770 with the development of canals, railways and steam-powered mills. Old workings, being shallow holes in the ground, are difficult to locate. But from 1760 collieries leave more traces: deep pits, impressive headstock and winding gear, railed-ways to town or port, miners' cottages. Winding gear, for instance, is at first a horse-windlass, then about 1790 a simple beam engine run by steam. Railed-ways for horse-drawn wagons have left clear tracks especially in the north-east: cuttings, embankments, possibly wooden and iron sleepers or rails.

Production of metallic iron demands the heating of ore with other materials like charcoal. Since the Iron Age men produced wrought iron for tools and weapons by direct reduction of ore on bloomery hearths (later with water-powered bellows) and this inefficient method has left greyish cinder heaps rich in iron. After 1490 the blast furnace with water-powered bellows was introduced to the Kent and Sussex Weald. A tall square stone-built structure, the furnace with enclosed hearth and great height allowed very high temperatures in the production of molten metal. Manufacturers built large dams across streams to provide sufficient head of water for bellows and forge hammers. Slag heaps lie all around and deeply rutted tracks lead to main roads or rivers.

In 1709 Abraham Darby of Coalbrookdale began working the coke-fired furnace for making cast-iron. Later came Cort's puddling process using a reverberatory furnace for production of coke-smelted wrought iron. Surviving early furnaces are usually stone-built, square at the base tapering to the top, powered by bellows. Nearby are forge-house and pool, stream and water-wheel. Hammers in the forge may have been worked by water since medieval days.

Since early times steel had been produced by the cementation process. Wrought iron and charcoal, heated in closed clay pots in a cone-shaped furnace, yielded blister steel. Huntsman's crucible process, from the mid-eighteenth century, improved on this, using closed fireclay crucibles and intense heat in a coke-fired furnace to manufacture cast steel.

Waterways

The improvement of rivers and the building of canals gave

the country an excellent system of waterways by about 1820. Some waterways catered for coastal traffic, others merely for tiny tub-boats. Public companies generally undertook the construction and management of these works, though branch lines to collieries or factories would be built by factory owners themselves.

Near villages and factories stand wharves for transhipment of goods like coal, machines or grain. There is often evidence of wooden posts in the bank; a paved track or railed-way; a warehouse; and an inn. Nearby may lie a canal basin or harbour for one or two boats, or even a boat-building yard.

Make measured sketches of all waterway bridges, tunnels and aqueducts. It is exciting to find the canal itself running in clay-filled or iron troughs over roads or streams. Notice that early tunnels had no internal towpaths. Either boatmen or full-time leggers, lying on their backs, kicked the boat through. Their horses walked over the tunnel top.

Railways

Railways have changed the face of the landscape on a grand scale. As railed roads for horse wagons they probably started in Nottinghamshire in 1604, spread to mining districts like Tyneside and Shropshire during the eighteenth century and with the advent of steam began to cover all the country from 1830. Railways were built by mining companies for the movement of their own goods. But in some cases a line was laid down by speculators who opened the track to all toll-payers. From 1830 a few industrialists built private lines, mainly within factory premises, but most work was undertaken by public companies.

Rail trackways are most readily recognisable, even where the line had been abandoned by 1800. Look for the tell-tale lane or hedge that leads from mine or mill to canal or village following a former railed-way. Sleepers and rails are of wood, iron or stone, many designs being tried prior to 1810. Survey also stone or cast-iron bridges, tunnels, cuttings and embankments. Some of these works stopped up ancient roads, divided fields and farms in two and littered the country with spoil banks. Try to record all buildings such as stations, signal-boxes, station houses, even lamp-posts. Go into details: furnishing of waiting room, manufacturer and style of water-closets, size of ticket office, telegraph installation and lighting.

Railway building convulsed the country with enormous embankments, cuttings, tunnels, viaducts, destruction of houses and erection of taverns, stations, warehouses. Some of the monuments are so familiar that we consider them as natural features but where did the earth for embankments come from and how was the work organised? J. Simmons in *The Railways of Britain* (1968) deals with these topics. There is a gazetteer of railed-ways in B. Baxter *Stone Blocks and Iron Rails* (1966).

7. GENTLE INTRODUCTION TO DOCUMENTS

Original documents must support any history that is to be worthwhile. Most manuscripts relating to all villages and towns have never been printed in any book, not even in summary form. So for your next job seek out this unique material from many repositories throughout Britain.

As a gentle introduction to documents go to your local repository. This may be the library (for instance the Bodleian at Oxford or Sheffield City for south Yorkshire). It is most likely to be the county record office. A list of these appears in the appendix. There are national centres in London like the Public Record Office, Chancery Lane; the British Museum; or Society of Friends Library. Sometimes relevant documents still lie in the diocesan record office, at the estate office or muniment room of your local landowner, in the attics of an old-established solicitor, at the council office or parish church.

County record office

The English and Welsh county record office was established to preserve the great heritage of manuscript material scattered throughout every shire. Most offices developed out of the department of the clerk of the peace, officer in charge of quarter sessions records. To these documents have been added legal, parish, county, family, diocesan, business, school and probate collections. Each collection of documents is known as an archive. The head of the county's archives is the county archivist.

The county archivist collects documents from wherever these are stored: parish church, country mansion, factory, estate office. He usually accepts deposits on terms of permanent loan. Manuscripts may be discovered in waterlogged cellars of solicitors or rat-infested attics of council offices and as a result can be in a deplorable state on their arrival in the record office. The archivist cleans and dries out decayed papers or parchments before starting a preliminary sorting. Some material is so badly damaged that it has to be handed to the skilled repairs technician who, with correct and delicate tools and material, makes good the ravages of centuries. This job often takes many months.

Manuscripts need then to be fully sorted, calendared and boxed. The detailed abstract or calendar so produced is used by students as a catalogue to save searching through every document in a collection. Archival material is stored in a properly designed strongroom, proof against rats, fire, damp, insects and careless students. Calendars are placed on open shelves in the students' search room. Here also may be consulted reference works on national and local history, genealogy, archives and palaeography. Sometimes there is a card index of persons, places and subjects referred to in documents.

Choose from the index or calendars any document that interests you just to get an idea of what archival material looks like. Ask the county archivist if the document is available: it may be in the process of detailed calendaring or repair. The various processes that a document collection goes through in a record office take months, even years, and it is unfair to hurry an archivist by complaining. In the search room use pencil for writing because ink may mark a document that is unique and priceless. Have clean hands. Never smoke, eat or talk loudly in the search room. A document is not loaned out, of course, because usually only one copy exists in the whole world, and this is uniquely valuable.

The skilled and specialist staff of a county record office always provides interested service to help you choose a subject for research and a list of documents most readily available for your purpose. Never hesitate to ask because you can save yourself a lot of time and worry. But archivists do not have the time to complete your research for you.

Public Record Office

In 1838 the government set up the Public Record Office in Chancery Lane to care for all state records. The oldest public record is Domesday Book of 1086. Then follow documents of the king's household and of the treasurer. The real starting point is the year 1199 when the government began preserving copies of all letters and charters despatched outwards by the chancellor. Since then millions of documents have been created and preserved by all government departments. Every English community is mentioned somewhere in this mass.

Calendars or printed copies of many documents can be consulted at libraries. The Stationery Office issues a free list of publications (HMSO Sectional List 24).

Palaeography

Palaeography means old writing. The inability to read old writing may at first prove a hindrance in your work. If you can learn to tackle slovenly modern hands, however, you will certainly eventually read old documents. In the past many people learned writing as an art under severe masters and consequently tended to follow set patterns. With practice you can distinguish hands of all centuries from Domesday onwards. Unfortunately many manuscripts are in medieval Latin, which was in general use in legal records till 1733, or in Norman French. If you do not read these languages ask your local archivist for aid. You will soon learn many key words.

There are some excellent helps in the palaeographical field. Use Hilda Grieve *Examples of English Handwriting 1150-1750,* with transcripts and translations (1954). See an article in *Amateur Historian* volume 7, number 3 (1966) by K. C. Newton 'Reading Medieval Local Records' (reprinted from volume 3, number 2). A collection of abbreviations, Latin words and names used in English historical manuscripts and records is found in C. T. Martin *Record Interpreter.* R. E. Latham *Revised Medieval Latin Word-List* (1965) is essential.

Dating

During Saxon and Norman times the new year began on 25th December. From about 1190 to 1751 Lady Day, 25th March, started the year. Only from 1752 did England revert to the Roman date of 1st January. If your document is dated 1751 or earlier and relates to any day between 1st January and 24th March, take care. What we should call 29th January 1649 is 29th January 1648 by old-style counting. People were in 1648 until 25th March. Modern historians often write this '29th January 1648/49' to save confusion.

8. MAPS

Maps and plans are perhaps the clearest and certainly the most informative of all sources for local history. These should be studied and copied before all other records. Take the copies with you during walks about your territory. Notice features that have changed over the years as well as the more permanent landmarks like parish church, castle hill and roads. Maitland in *Domesday Book and Beyond* as early as 1897 considered 'two little fragments' of the one-inch Ordnance map to be 'more eloquent than would be many paragraphs of written discourse'. So begin with Ordnance maps.

Ordnance Survey

Ordnance maps are essential sources for many historical subjects. Place-names that have since disappeared are recorded on nineteenth-century maps while archaeological features lost under housing estates may be recognised. The scale is sufficiently large for the indication of most points of interest in a village.

The Board of Ordnance began its survey in 1795 and the one-inch to the mile map of Kent appeared in 1801. This series continued with maps of the south-east of England and the West Country, the Midlands, Wales, and the North so that by 1840 the whole country south of a line from Preston to Hull was surveyed. Manuscript surveyors' drawing from the one-inch survey of 1795-1873, showing more detail than the printed maps are in the British Museum Map Room.

Then as a result of public demand for maps on a scale larger than one-inch the Board of Ordnance initiated a six-inch survey first in Ireland in 1824, then in northern England (1840), finally in Scotland (1843). An even larger scale was adopted after much dispute in 1853 when surveyors began the twenty-five-inch to the mile plan of County Durham. This survey had covered all England and Wales (except uncultivated lands) by 1893.

A town map of St. Helens on a scale of five feet to one mile was published in 1843-4, and this successful project initiated a fifty-year programme during which many British towns were surveyed in great detail. Scales vary from five to ten feet to the mile.

Ordnance maps are an essential starting point for village history because they provide a picture of the district at a number of dates from the beginning of the nineteenth century onwards. Even if you are studying Saxon or medieval topics a map of 1840 can help to show what the place looked like before sweeping Victorian changes. The pattern of open fields quite often survived until Ordnance Survey times.

For a full guide to ordnance maps including a key to what is available for every area of Britain see *The Historian's Guide to Ordnance Survey Maps* by J. B. Harley and C. W. Phillips (1965). Older maps are usually held by the county record office, library or surveyor's department of the local county or borough council. Copies can be had from the Ordnance Survey Office in Southampton. The first edition one-inch is now published in facsimile. More recent editions, including an excellent survey on a scale of $2\frac{1}{2}$ inches, should be purchased for use while investigating local history.

Tithe maps

Tithe maps are excellent parish and township surveys produced at the time when church tithes in kind (hay, pigs, eggs)
were commuted into money payments, usually after 1836. The
process of commutation demands a village meeting to agree
on the value of tithes and the terms acceptable to all parties.
Minute-books of meetings may usefully survive in parish-church
collections or at solicitors. Then an award of rent charge is
made which has to be shared among all proprietors. So there
becomes necessary the accurate large-scale village or town map,
known as the tithe map, to show every parcel of land, every
road, path, house, shop, stream, every inch of ground in the
township. The scale can be twenty-five inches to the mile and
most maps are coloured. The tithe map is frequently the earliest
township map, especially in northern England, though some
places commuted tithes prior to 1836 and possess no plans.

The key to this map is the apportionment in which are
named owners and occupiers of every parcel of land. Acreage
and tithe payments appear against each parcel. Apportionment,
award and map are sealed and then fixed together. The document provides a picture of many places about 1840 just before
the great changes of Victorian days. It shows land ownership,
state of cultivation, name of occupiers of property, size of
estates, routes of canals and railways, number of farms and
houses, traces of old earthworks and medieval cultivation,
names of woods, lanes, closes, commons and houses, in all an
unrivalled survey of town and village. There are three copies
of every tithe map and apportionment. One is at the Public
Record Office, another at the diocesan registry (usually now
the county record office), the third in the parish chest.

Printed maps

Most printed maps prior to 1810 are on too small a scale to
be really useful. Printed county maps have been on sale since
Elizabeth Tudor's reign. Only the one-inch maps can indicate
an area in any detail but even the smallest occasionally show in
one corner an enlarged plan of an important town. Some plans
are the bird's eye view type so popular in Tudor and Stuart
days. They do indicate lay-out of streets and fields, size of
houses, place-names and some industries. A number of oblique
and bird's eye views of British towns drawn about 1560-87 and
1611 appears in Braun and Hogenberg *Civitates Orbis Terrarum*
(facsimile edition 1966).

Only a few towns like London and Norwich can boast of
sixteenth-century printed town plans. But a landmark in
cartography is the inclusion by John Speed in his *Theatre of the*

Empire of Great Britaine . . . (1612) of seventy-three town plans and views. Salisbury, Buckingham, Ipswich and Nottingham are all represented. Eighteenth-century plans are accurate, large-scale and often colourful.

The availability of Ordnance and the tithe maps after 1840 effectively limited the use of privately printed maps. J. B. Harley *Maps for the Local Historian* (1972) concisely summarises all relevant sources and sets out such useful details as the towns surveyed by Speed. Most libraries and record offices can produce a varied selection of local maps. The British Museum owns an unrivalled collection, to which there is a printed index.

Maps created by inquiries

Many maps have been produced as a result of government curiosity or to help in a law case. Thus in the sixteenth century the Tudors ordered strategic towns to be surveyed in detail. Defences were clearly shown. These maps survive at the British Museum (Cottonian MSS) and Public Record Office (State Papers). There are lists of these sets of documents. Look also at the alphabetical descriptive list of *Maps and plans in the Public Record Office relating to the British Isles c. 1410-1860* (1967). These maps were either used in court cases or preserved for the information of government departments.

Enclosure maps

Enclosure of open fields, moorland or meadow, all at one time common land, has long been a feature of the English economy. Enclosure merits a section of its own in any local history, and references to the far-reaching effects of the process are found in many types of record. The map and award often produced at enclosure time provide a good survey of your township and should be examined at this early stage of research. Consult the parliamentary Return of Inclosure Acts in *House of Commons Sessional Papers,* 1914, lxvii, to learn if your parish was affected. General acts have been passed since 1801 to facilitate enclosure. There is a printed alphabetical *Index of Local and Personal Acts 1801-1947.*

Documents which are likely to be of most use date from about 1740. Each enclosure document whether rolled or in book form consists of an award that sets out exactly the disposition of all affected common land. Not only farmers and freeholders but the poor and the parson obtain portions. There may also be available the minute-book of the inclosure commissioners, with letters, agreements and sketches. If you are lucky

37

a map will accompany the award to show where all the enclosures are situated. Some surveyors show a plan of the entire village, not merely the common, in order to mark the property in respect of which allotments are claimed. You know exactly from numbers on the map which land is taken by each inhabitant. What has happened to these allotments?

Look especially for old versions of place-names, ancient lanes, new access roads, houses erected in the enclosures, signs of medieval farming, land given to charities, poor, parson and school. Try to work out which men were losing, which gaining from enclosure.

To find out where maps and awards are held today consult the county archivist. The county record office usually possesses a copy of enclosure documents made after 1740 but some are in the Public Record Office or the parish chest.

---

9. ESTATE PAPERS

English townships have usually formed part of some large estate and much information can be found in estate papers of the various landowners whether local squire, monastery, industrial company or Oxford college. Landed proprietors, however, may own hundreds of acres or just a single house. Even the latter is an estate with its own documents. A village can be owned by one man or be entirely in the possession of resident freeholders. By seeking papers relating to all properties you provide a sound basis for a complete history.

Begin by discovering what estates are spread about your locality. Your reading will probably have supplied some clues. The county archivist will tell of other estates that have long since disappeared and can indicate where relevant papers may be found. Many archives will already be deposited at the county record office. Alternatively you read reports of the Historical Manuscripts Commission, which was established in 1869 to report in some detail on manuscript collections of historical importance in private hands. It now has two offshoots:

1. The National Register of Archives has listed about eleven thousand document collections dating from every century.

2. The Manorial and Tithe Documents Registers record the whereabouts of manorial and tithe documents.

There is an index of persons mentioned in all reports from 1870 to 1957 published by the Stationery Office (1935-66). Reports themselves are available in libraries. For further enquiries write to the Secretary, Historical Manuscripts Commission, Quality Court, Chancery Lane, London WC2.

Estate maps

Among the most useful of estate papers are maps and plans. These show the property of one landowner who had employed a surveyor to indicate the extent and important features of the estate. If your chosen area has been divided among many proprietors at one time or another, then you may expect to find a number of maps showing sections of the township. Your record office usually produces a list of estate maps.

Maps may be of all sizes, big rolls of parchment or small pieces of paper, wonderfully coloured or merely etched in black and white. At times the surveyor draws a whole district or village but often leaves blank spaces where land does not belong to his employer. Do not assume this is waste land. Estate maps first appear in any number in the sixteenth century and continue to be produced until rendered obsolete by Ordnance maps.

Surveys

A survey is a word picture of an estate, dating from about 1540-1720, giving information in several forms:

John Swanne owns one close called Big Heye 0-2-31 adjoyneinge Northe on the Common, northeaste on widow Bell's croft, south and west on Westfield furlong.

Term for 3 lives	Description	Tenant	Acreage
	messuage	William Thompson	0-0-20

Rentals and leases

Rentals and leases are complementary documents. I have traced one estate cottage and garden back to 1520 with no more than a good set of these records. I followed tenants' names in the rent books beginning at the latest date and working back. When one man disappeared, say in 1777, I looked at 1776 for another person who paid the same rent for a cottage and garden. Then to make certain I examined leases for 1776-77 to find the authority by which one tenant replaced the other.

Title deeds

Without further ado try to see title deeds relating to each property in the township. Every piece of ground ought to be represented in someone's deeds. Some lands will be named with hundreds of other acres in comprehensive deeds of a large land-owner. Quite small gardens may have title deeds of their own stretching back some centuries. It may be possible to obtain full lists of owners and occupiers over the centuries, descriptions of different properties, place-names and family histories from a careful examination of deeds.

Deeds of title include any document that has been used to prove ownership to property. Most owners have kept deeds bundled together to ensure that none strays. These documents were drawn up to give legal evidence of Brown's disposal of property to Smith on such and such a day. They were noi intended to provide a history of village estates and their rambling legal style may at first defy understanding. Lawyers retained Latin in some cases until 1733. On the other hand deeds when treated intelligently form a firm basis of research.

For fuller guides to the use of title deeds see an excellent pamphlet obtainable from Birmingham University Extra-Mural Studies Department by Julian Cornwall *How to read old title deeds XVI-XIX Centuries* (1964).

The simplest type of deed relates to one compact property which has long been freehold. One man sells and another buys the whole, and so on through the centuries. As you work through bundles of deeds you might make a full calendar, or abstract, of each document but this is not essential. It is, however, vital to note the names of all parties to the deed, their places of residence and jobs, an exact description of all lands and date. Conditions of sale and price paid may be useful.

1. Miles Geldart of Carlton, yeoman, to
2. George Swann of Mellmerby, cordwainer
   – all that Messuage or Dwelling House scituate and being in Carlton aforesaid called or known by the name of St. Thomas Chappell – 4 May 1681.

This basic information leads to further research. When did Geldart buy the house? Why should Swann from another village purchase the place? What does the name tell about the original use of the land?

In many deeds there may be a fourth factor to notice: the 'whereas' clause. Lawyers often quote back to previous deeds partly to show that the seller's title was good, and this practice is invaluable where older deeds have been lost.

There may be a fifth factor: a detailed plan of the farm, house, shop or estate which is drawn on the deed itself. Plans usually date from after 1800.

Where do you find deeds? First try the homes of various village property owners. Deeds may be in their sideboards or under the carpet, at the bank or with the solicitor. Some owners have deposited documents on loan with a county record office. If the property forms part of a large estate deeds will be tucked away among estate muniments.

In Middlesex and the Ridings of Yorkshire there existed four deeds registries. Established between 1704 and 1736 these offices copied out essential facts from every deed that concerns property in those counties, indexing by name and place. Record offices now shelve surviving registers.

Notices and particulars of sale

Notices of sale of houses, land and personal goods were often inserted in local newspapers or nailed on walls before the property was disposed of. Conditions and particulars of sale with plans also appear at this stage though these were to be consulted at the local solicitor's, estate agents or nearest inn. These documents are boldly printed on paper and dozens of copies may survive. In one small collection I found notices dating from 1705 onwards advertising the sale of a farm, tolls of a turnpike road and the office of parish tithe farmer (in return for a fixed rent to the rector he got what profit he could from collecting tithes). Most surviving notices are in family muniments at the solicitor's or county record office. Copies are, of course, in old newspapers.

---

10. TOWN BOOKS

The township has since Tudor times been the basic administrative unit of English local government. It does not necessarily cover the same area as parish or manor, though manor court and parish vestry meeting had a hand in its governance. Thriving townships might contain several ecclesiastical parishes and, by obtaining a charter of rights and duties, become boroughs or cities. Northern townships within vast parishes ran their own affairs with a town meeting. In the lowlands parish and town may coincide: here the vestry governs each community. Victorian reforms created other local units like urban and rural districts, civil parishes and county boroughs.

The term 'town books' is adopted for all local government records. Documents may start in the fourteenth century. For a guide to local village administration see W. E. Tate *The Parish Chest* (1969).

Town books remain the property of the authority which first created them. Thus most village and town documents are

41

in the church safe. In large villages containing many townships each place might keep its own records and these have survived in the hands of the parish clerk or of descendants of former township officers. Boroughs have often built their own muniment room at the town hall or guildhall. Most authorities were however affected by local government reorganisation and records may well have found their way since then to the central library or record office of each new county or district.

Conurbations of recent growth like Manchester possess records only from the date of borough incorporation. Prior to this each constituent township of the built-up area had its own administration and records. Documents may lie in the old church of each village or in private hands. But usually city librarians and archivists have collected records diligently into one central repository.

Manorial records

Manorial organisation was superimposed prior to the Conquest on communities already divided into estates of varying size. The lord of the manor held courts for his manorial people at regular intervals, often every fortnight.

The most interesting manorial documents date from the period 1220-1720. Court documents may be held by anyone who has owned the manor. Sometimes solicitors act as custodians. Manuscripts are protected by law, and many owners have deposited them in county record offices. The Public Record Office published a useful list of court rolls in its possession in 1896. See page 38 on the Manorial Documents Registry.

Often written on pieces of parchment which were then stitched together and rolled like pipes, usually in Latin, court rolls begin with place and date and continue with lists of local jurors. These jurors present cases for the lord's consideration and wrongdoers are duly punished. Any kind of village problem can come to court: scouring ditches, stray cattle on cornfields, witchcraft, assault, theft, disputes about boundary stones, rents, the lord's corn-mill. In one Whitby (Yorkshire) roll William Ward is fined 'for emptying his Chamberpot into the common highstreet to the detriment of the populace'.

Court records include extents of the manorial estate. These describe the bounds of the lord's land, mentioning features of the district like trees, cottages and new enclosures from the waste. Very useful also will be manor court surrenders of property on the death or departure of one tenant and the admittance of his successor. The tenants would hold copies of the court roll to record this transaction. In any case the court book or roll fully describes the change, and tenants therefore hold by copy of court roll. I have traced one east Lancashire copyhold farm in these surrenders from 1910 back to 1582.

Custumals set out the customs of the manor. Tenants' privileges and duties are laid down so that the manor might be administered smoothly. Here you can see the community's daily routine, most especially in Tudor and Stuart times.

Minutes

A meeting of parishioners in the vestry of the church or a town meeting at the inn governed most places. Incorporated towns had their mayor and council. In all cases minutes of meetings in volumes or on scraps of paper were usually kept by a clerk who also dealt with petitions and correspondence. Documents may date from about 1320. They deal with every local problem imaginable: sewers, town common, repair of parish church or grammar school, witches, trade, apprenticeship, smoking chimneys, rights of freemen, parliamentary representation. The decisions which altered the course of local history were taken at these vestry and borough council meetings.

Rate and account books

The administration of villages and towns demanded the collection of rates on property so that essential local services might be performed. Not all documents are in book form, but the presentation of information is similar in all cases. The relevant officer makes a list of all sources of income. This quite often turns into an annual house by house directory because each property is listed in order. Then in account books the local officers explain all expenditure: to the surveyor 'for repaireing longbrigd £2 7s'; to the overseer of the poor '3s 6d per Weeke for Jane Cooke's Bastard'; to the constable 'for Whipping a vagrant etc. 4d'. Rate books are usually listed at the record office. Most begin no earlier than about 1690.

Settlement and removal

After 1662 everyone was supposed to have a legal place of settlement. When a person wished to go and live elsewhere he had to go armed with a settlement certificate stating his place of settlement. To this place he would be removed by a magistrate's order if he seemed likely to be a charge on the rates. Some examinations taken prior to removal furnish place of birth and marriage, towns of residence and work over twenty years or more, age and occupation. These types of documents may be in both quarter sessions records and the parish chest.

1694 Tax

In 1694 Parliament laid a tax on births, marriages, burials, bachelors over 25 and childless widowers. The impost survived till 1706. Each parish was supposed to exhibit a complete list of all inhabitants by households. Parents, children, servants, lodgers are named. Some lists provide details of jobs, addresses and approximate value of real and personal estate because the tax was graduated according to social and economic status. Thus these documents may be the earliest of census returns. Only a few documents now remain, mainly in local record offices.

Apprenticeship

Most local collections contain apprenticeship registers and deeds. Young people, especially paupers and orphans, were apprenticed perhaps as butchers or shoemakers for a period of years. The apprenticeship deed is written out twice, one copy for master, one for parish or parent. The single sheet of paper on which copies are inscribed head to head is cut with an indented line to separate the texts. This produces the indenture. Each deed will give the name, age and parentage of the child; his residence; name and job of his master; and the date.

Charities

Many charities have been founded by private and public benefactors to provide comforts for old and young. For histories of charities like schools, almshouses and donations of money or food see the abstract of the returns concerning charitable donations, published 1816, and the relevant report of the commissioners for inquiries concerning charities in England and Wales dated between 1819 and 1837, all in *Commons Sessional Papers*. There is an index in *Sessional Papers* for 1840 (279), xix, pt. II.

Court books

Large boroughs established courts with judicial and administrative functions. These courts had varied names: mayor's court, pie-powder court, petty view and court of assembly. The magistrates heard cases of assault, illegal trading, insanitary habits and so on. Rules were made for the better governance of the town. Proceedings, minutes and orders are often found on loose parchments as well as in hefty volumes. Some records date from the thirteenth century. Borough archives also contain manorial court records. Perhaps the lord had himself granted the borough charter. Later, most boroughs acquired the right to hold their own courts of quarter sessions.

Estate documents

Communities own property. So are created estate records of value for the topographical, genealogical and economic history of the township. Deeds of title running to millions lie in council strongrooms, with leases, maps, accounts, surveys and letters interspersed.

Improvement commissioners' records

Improvement commissioners were appointed by parliament to develop town streets, lighting, paving and sewage from the eighteenth century. Records, which are usually with borough or city archives today, throw light on the struggles of the first town planners against wretched living conditions. Powers of commissioners passed to local councils in later Victorian days.

Guild records

Tradesmen, merchants and craftsmen have since early Norman times formed within corporate towns an association known as the guild merchant. To this any member of the burghal community could belong regardless of occupation. Members were free of local tolls and were given a monopoly of trading save in victuals. Documents of the guild deal with every aspect of local economic affairs as will be evident if you study Charles Gross *The Gild Merchant* (1890). Original guild records are usually with borough archives at the guildhall.

During the thirteenth century craft guilds grew up in large towns to cater for individual trades like weavers, silversmiths and fishmongers. Often fiercely opposed to the policies of guild merchants and town corporations, the craft companies retained their own records. What survives may still be in the hands of the individual companies, though sixty London livery companies have deposited records at the Guildhall Library.

---

11. CHURCH ARCHIVES

Because the various church authorities have for centuries concerned themselves with every aspect of human affairs documents so created cannot be overlooked by the local historian even when religion as such does not figure in the study. The bishop as head of the diocese has created records of great complexity which survive from the thirteenth century. There are also estate records for the landed property of bishops and cathedral chapters. Documents in the parish chest may begin in the fourteenth century.

Bishop's registers

Bishop's registers are the oldest diocesan records dating back to 1209 at Lincoln. Contents are various, including records of consecrations of churches, institutions to benefices and cases of clerical misbehaviour. For your parish-church story these documents are essential reading. Some registers are printed by the Canterbury and York Society. The handwriting and Latin of unprinted registers is very difficult.

Diocesan papers

The registrar of each diocese preserved thousands of routine papers concerning clergymen and churches. You can follow a clergyman's career from entering the ministry to his burial and probate of his will. Licences to incumbents for non-residence, to schoolteachers, surgeons, midwives, parish clerk and curates can be found. Building, repairing, altering and demolishing all church property is well documented. Papers may date from as early as 1500.

Bishop's returns

The Privy Council sent to all the bishops in 1563 queries concerning the state of dioceses. These included requests for the number of households in each parish. The surviving returns are in British Museum Harleian Manuscripts.

Bishop Compton's Return of 1676 concerns much of the Midlands and South. The information includes numbers of Anglicans, papists and dissenters in each parish and is the basis for population estimates. The William Salt Library, Stafford, possesses a copy of the return.

Bishop's visitation records

A bishop was supposed to travel round his diocese at not too infrequent intervals. Prior to the visit queries were sent out to determine the state of each parish. Most were duly answered by incumbents or clerks and filed in the diocesan registry. Surviving documents mostly date from the eighteenth and nineteenth centuries and are now in the county record office acting as diocesan registry.

The bishop naturally wanted to know whether the incumbent was resident or not; value and age of church plate; date of registers. Such facts give a good picture of church organisation. But other queries include the number of families in the parish; numbers of nonconformists; strength of Methodist Sunday schools; main employment opportunities in the district; charities; extent and description of farms and fields owned by the church authorities.

Diocesan terriers

A terrier is a list of all the landed possessions of a church. Generally the document begins with a description of the church itself, its fabric and furnishings and of the churchyard. Then parsonage and garden are sufficiently surveyed to enable the researcher to picture the place clearly. Any other outbuildings and cottages belonging to the church are mentioned in this way: 'a mere cottage built with clay walls and covered with thatch containing 3 rooms' (1604).

Terriers rarely date from before the seventeenth century. Some are written in Latin, some in English. Documents vary in size and clarity according to clerk or incumbent. Terriers survive both in the parish chest and in the bishop's own records at the diocesan registry.

Diocesan court and cause papers

The bishop's (or consistory) court dealt with a wide variety of ecclesiastical offences: indiscipline of clergy, tithes, matrimony, probate of wills. Depositions in cause papers mention such questions as farming practices, parish bounds, ancient charters, local customs, trading and family history. Documents usually date from the early fifteenth to the late nineteenth centuries. Most papers will have to be examined in the original because few calendars or editions are yet available. Documents are at the diocesan registry. Look at J. S. Purvis *Introduction to Ecclesiastical Records* (1953) and D. M. Owen *The Records of the Established Church in England* (1970) for some guide before you start researching into these difficult but vastly rewarding records.

Diocesan faculties and consecrations

Papers concerning the issue of faculties and consecration deeds deal with church alterations, monuments, private pews and building of galleries or new churches.

Bishop's transcripts

After the church injunction of 1597 each parish clerk was to send to the bishop a transcript of the entries in the parish register of baptisms, marriages and burials. These documents, usually of parchment, are signed by the incumbent and churchwardens. Their value lies in their being a substitute for missing, illegible or damaged parish registers. Most transcripts date from 1598 to 1837. They are usually now in the county record office.

Diocesan marriage bonds

Sometimes a couple obtained a bishop's licence to wed when

banns were not, for some reason, convenient. Prior to granting the licence diocesan authorities made enquiries and took statements concerning the two parties. Bonds and allegations, possibly dating from the sixteenth century, often show the couple's abode, age ('over 21') and occupation. Place of intended marriage and names of sureties also appear. Marriage bonds are in the county record office where some indexes are available.

Probate records

Ecclesiastical authorities took charge of proving wills in medieval times and continued to do so until 1858. Hence early wills needed in your survey should be sought in diocesan record offices or in courts of peculiars (a district exempt from jurisdiction of the bishop in whose diocese it lies). Most inhabitants of your village prove wills in the court of the local bishop, though owners of property over a wide area of England and Wales looked to the courts at York or Canterbury. The locating of wills is in any case not difficult if you know in what district a person died or owned property. To learn where the will is likely to be deposited nowadays consult J. S. W. Gibson *Wills and Where to Find them* (1974). Most collections of wills are in county record offices.

Wills are essential sources of local history:

1. The testator will doubtless mention his friends, relations and neighbours. This is useful in proving relationships within a community. Notice how men try to build up business empires or large estates through intermarriage. You may wonder why the dead man left so much to 'Jane Bousfield my servant'.

2. A will may serve as a title deed.

3. Wills describe property in very useful terms: 'my Messuage or Dwelling House with my new Stable and the Rooms over the same now used as a dwellinghouse and occupied by . . . '; 'all that my Meadow called Salthousemead'.

4. A will provides information on commercial, farming and industrial interests of the testator. The factory is described in detail. Heirs are instructed point by point how a handicraft shop is conducted. Business partners, debtors, creditors, customers are often named.

5. Until about 1740 inventories of the deceased's goods accompany a will: hay, wagons, clothes, utensils, furniture, all are listed and valued. Appraisers journey through the house room by room and describe every item in minute detail.

6. The will shows the value of the deceased's personalty.

Parish records

Documents of the Church of England parish may be in the church safe or chest; at the diocesan registry; or with the county record office on loan. The oldest records are likely to be vestry minutes and accounts, detailing decisions and finances of the incumbent, churchwardens and local worthies who administered church affairs. Documents of some town parishes begin in the fourteenth century. Information yielded includes church fabric repairs, graveyard upkeep, building of extensions, purchase of plate and vestments, all matters of immediate ecclesiastical importance. The vestry, of course, administered the parish as a civil unit also and documents in this case are discussed in chapter 10.

Parish registers of baptisms, marriages and burials were first produced under the provisions of Thomas Cromwell's mandate of 1538. Each vestry was to acquire a chest with locks and keys where a register book could be stored. The parish clerk entered details from notes or memory quite regularly. Early records, usually on paper and unbound, have not always survived and it was not till 1597 that the church injunction forced incumbents to use parchments bound in book form and to send a fair copy of entries yearly to the diocesan registry. From 1754 marriage entries are in a separate book on printed forms. Baptisms and burials appear on standard forms after 1813. Parish registers of the Church of England are still kept.

Researchers employ registers for genealogical purposes. It is instructive to work out the pedigrees of local families to explain perhaps the succession to property or the accumulation of capital. As an introduction read David Iredale *Discovering Your Family Tree* (revised edition 1977). People interested in population should first read *An Introduction to English Historical Demography* (1966) edited by E. A. Wrigley. This work shows how registers draw a picture of the family from about 1600 onwards by providing relationships, birth rate, age at marriage, incidence of plague and disease, mobility of families and so on. To obtain an approximate population figure count the number of baptisms over a decade and work out an annual average, then multiply by thirty.

By far the most authoritative work on church archives is the *National Index of Parish Registers* (Society of Genealogists, in course of publication). This will provide a guide on all surviving records. The first two volumes introduce sources of births, marriages and deaths before 1837. Later volumes deal in detail with Anglican and other records in each parish of England and Wales. Expertly written articles and excellent bibliography can hardly be faulted.

Other church records

Many communities have gained special character by the presence of people who refused to attend Anglican services. Registers, minute-books and correspondence of Roman Catholic, Methodist, Quaker, Baptist and other churches are sometimes found locally and are occasionally available in county record offices. Before embarking on research read the article on archives of the non-established churches in L. Redstone and F. W. Steer *Local Records* (1953). The 1851 census of religious worship at the Public Record Office shows the size of congregation on one Sunday in 1851 as well as the date when the place of worship was established.

School records

Education has for long been a church affair. Records of some grammar and village schools may well still be in the parish chest. Most schools and masters appear in diocesan and parish documents almost yearly from 1547 to about 1800. Three unlicensed 'infirm sailors' were discovered by the bishop to be teaching school at Northam in 1724.

The foundation charter or title deed should be sought first, perhaps at the school itself. Original deeds of many charity schools are enrolled on close rolls in the Public Record Office. Then look for log books, masters' diaries and correspondence because these provide daily summaries of school life.

12. QUARTER SESSIONS

From the sixteenth century magistrates in quarter and petty sessions have acted as judges in law cases and as administrators and keepers of records. Sessions documents in most counties are now in record offices and are so important and voluminous that your local history cannot be completed unless you have spent at least a year or so examining the records.

Judicial records

Law cases concern most types of offence: assault, theft, riot, bastardy, witchcraft and vagrancy. Many documents were brought into court as a result, dealt with and then threaded on a single file for permanent preservation. This forms the sessions bundle which must be examined document by document because comparatively few calendars yet exist. Among the bundles will be petitions for help in hard times from paupers, calendars of prisoners awaiting trial, depositions about stolen goods and indictments of towns for not repairing roads. The clerk of the peace kept a minute-book of proceedings. He noted in his order book the justices' decisions. Sessions records are generally in English from 1650 and not difficult to decipher.

Administrative records

Administrative duties of justices concerned bridges, militia, gaols, lunatics, roads, weights and measures, poor relief, vagrancy, the county rate, and so much more that some benches were almost crippled by the burden. Sessions files and separate books provide information on these activities.

The poor law occupied much time. Petitions from poor people asking for relief; from villages demanding money to erect a workhouse; from sailors needing help to return to their ships, all these are found. Magistrates ordered the removal of families to their place of legal settlement. The removal order names family members, providing ages and jobs and shows the two townships involved. Appeals by towns and families against these orders are numerous.

Supervision of inns and alehouses by magistrates started in Edward VI's reign but records are seldom earlier than 1640 and usually no earlier than 1780. Of course there may be scattered references in sessions bundles to unruly alehouses, thefts at inns and magistrates' meetings at hostelries. But for series of alehouse documents turn to recognisances 1640-1830 and to licensed victuallers' registers 1753-1828.

Registered and deposited records

Records deposited with the clerk of the peace for safe keeping include land taxes, electoral lists, maps, accounts and correspondence. Look in sessions records for the rules, lists of officers and accounts of your local savings bank (from 1817) or friendly societies (from 1793). The latter might be a charity for the poor or for education, a trade union group, a working men's club, a burial club or an insurance policy against sickness or unemployment. There are also details of bankrupts' estates. After the Napoleonic War accounts of turnpike road, gas and water companies were deposited yearly with the magistrates.

Under standing orders of the Commons, first made in 1792, whenever an authority planned public works like canals, railways, harbours or turnpiked roads the project had to be properly surveyed and a plan presented both to parliament and the clerk of the peace. These are the deposited plans. Such plans show the whole project, with ground plans, elevations and sections.

Road diversion records since 1697 and plans since 1773 have

at times been deposited with the clerk of the peace. There is usually a plan of the old and new roads with adjoining property delineated whether affected or not.

Parliament's distrust of dissenters from the Anglican church led to the registration of nonconformists' meeting. From the Toleration Act of 1688 to 1852 the clerk of the peace kept a register of buildings licensed as places of worship. You will find names of owners or occupiers, possibly names of members, denomination and addresses. Original returns from townships for a Commons inquiry of 1829 into nonconformist strength usually survive in county archives.

All boats on navigable rivers and canals were registered from 1795 to 1871. The magistrates also registered charities from 1786, gamekeepers from 1710 and printing presses, 1799-1869. By an act of 1795 people who used hair powder took out a one guinea certificate annually. Registers of duty-payers name local gentry and their servants together with those aspiring to genteel status like the parson.

Under an act of 1696 township constables were obliged to return every year to quarter sessions lists of men who were qualified to serve as jurors. These lists are in effect registers of local freeholders and therefore of electors in parliamentary elections. The constables might enter men's ages, occupations and places of abode. Lists of freeholders as such may survive for 1788-89, lists of jurors for 1696-1832.

In 1832 printed electoral lists begin. These yearly documents name all men qualified to vote for members of parliament. Women generally appear only after 1918, though a few could vote prior to this date in local elections. These lists are very useful in providing a voter's address and the address of the property in respect of which he claimed a vote. The history of a house, land and a family may be sought in these lists. By chance you may come across poll lists from the early eighteenth century to 1868 to tell you how people actually voted at various general elections.

Land tax returns may, if used with diligence, provide an excellent history of land ownership from as early as 1692 to 1831. Parliament granted the new king, William III, a tax on such property as houses, land, tithes and public offices to enable him to make war. Valuers surveyed all property and the king got a varying proportion of total annual value each year. The tax came more and more from landed property as years passed.

Every spring returns were made to local magistrates who were responsible for sending abstracts and money to London. Some justices preserved original tax lists in their own family muniments until 1780. But between 1780 and 1831 returns were supposed to be sent to the clerk of the peace to satisfy electoral registration regulations. These returns, possibly with earlier ones, are in the county record office nowadays. Documents are simple in form.

LAND TAX 1828

OWNER	OCCUPIER	PROPERTY	TAX PAID	TAX REDEEMED
William Leigh	Mary Guest	Cottage and garden	0–0–9½	0–0–9½
John & Matthew Ledward	Themselves	Smithy & house	0–1–6¾	– – –

Your first impression of land taxes may be: 'interesting but nothing special'. Yet if you can spare some weeks to examine lists year by year these documents are among the most useful for your purpose. I have copied all land taxes for my village from 1731 to 1831, put results side by side and so have a perfect chart of owners, occupiers, changes in property ownership, new houses, old dwellings demolished, Apart from the card index of persons this twelve-feet long list is my most valuable aid during research. The process needs some explaining, and you should read David Iredale *Discovering Your Old House* (Shire Publications, 1977) for the only current guide to this.

---

13. BUSINESS RECORDS

When you have a list of all the businesses that existed in your area during your chosen period select the firms that survive and seek documents from the present proprietors. Should the business no longer continue, the owners of the site may have records. County record offices are building up collections of business documents. Consult the Historical Association's pamphlet on *Business History* and the journal *Business History*.

Public undertakings

Canals, rivers, railways and roads are usually rich in records. Each project is likely to produce plans, accounts, letters, title deeds and leases, both prior to actual building and then regularly until cessation of operation. Archives of many railways and other transport undertakings are at the British Railways Board Historical Records Office. In some cases the company itself has retained old records. In others, archives centres have taken over: the University of Bristol library now possesses the Brunel manuscripts. Some collections are in the hands of firms of solicitors whose partners were once clerks or treasurers to the companies.

Tradesmen and industry

Tradesmen like cobblers or carpenters usually kept some accounts and bills though these rarely survive unless the enterprise prospered and expanded. Most local industries prosper and then decay, their records disappearing too. Their history will be got only from township records and estate papers. Records of these firms may well have been stored in the manager's head to save clerical work, competitors' piracy and government snooping. Documents have generally been destroyed or kept by a local attorney.

On the other hand business documents can be revealing not merely about the business itself but about many sides of village life. The older records of Samuel Courtauld and Company, textile manufacturers, preserved in Essex Record Office, tell much about wages, working conditions, business prospects and local politics.

Fire insurance records

Many premises have been insured against fire since Stuart times. Original policies survive in some private collections and describe the property in some detail. People also fixed a numbered and distinctive plaque called a fire-mark to their walls and this gives you your clue. Take a structure insured with the Sun Fire company and provided with a fire-mark showing the pattern of a sun on it. The number can be looked up in company records (now in the Guildhall Library in London) to indicate names of insurers and description of property over the years.

Solicitors' accumulations

English solicitors or attorneys often served as depositories for estate, business, official, manorial and parochial documents before the days of record offices. Local landowners, statutory authorities and industries employed solicitors as estate agents or clerks. Documents were created in and preserved at the solicitor's office. Here they have remained unless sent to the county archives. You can find every kind of record at the solicitor's: wills, land taxes, correspondence, surveys, deeds, maps. In one office I came upon several pre-Conquest charters; in another I found a series of the county coroner's records, 1806-88.

It is, however, not usually easy to discover which solicitors at present hold documents relating to your area. Solicitors themselves rarely know the extent of their holdings. My investigations combine clues from directories and law lists, requests to the county archivist and enquiries in the neighbourhood itself.

The law business itself may possess old records relating to its own activities especially correspondence, accounts, diaries and drafts of legal cases. These reveal the widespread influence of attorneys in the financial, commercial, landed and business fields.

14. GOVERNMENT RECORDS

The local historian should, near the end of his research, consult government records that are mainly in the Public Record Office, London. Documents date back some nine hundred years. Access is limited to searchers with reader's tickets but these are easily obtained by filling in a form stating name, address and purpose of research. The form is to be signed by a person of repute in your community. Photocopies of records can of course be obtained by post without the ticket if you cannot travel to London.

In order to find out which records will help your project consult the *Guide to the Contents of the Public Record Office* (1963–). Sectional list 24 issued by HMSO states what record office calendars of documents are already in print, for study in your local library. The List and Index Society is copying calendars from the search room of the record office, and again this will save your time in London. But remember that reading many public records demands a knowledge of Latin and palaeography.

Exchequer

The Exchequer was the department where appeared the king's debtors. It was also a court of law for revenue affairs. The office took its name from the chequered cloth on which officials performed their calculations prior to the introduction of Arabic numerals. Records of receipts begin in 1129.

During 1086 royal commissioners questioned the lords and tenants of English manors about ownership and extent of properties. The survey so produced is by far the earliest documentary record of most places in the country. Unfortunately the four northern counties are not surveyed, and Yorkshire and Lancashire are very hastily recorded in this Domesday survey. The West Country and East Anglia appear in great detail.

Domesday is primarily a personal inquiry into those holding land in chief of the king together with a full picture of each of their manors at the end of five hundred years of English settlement. The unit is the manor, possibly embracing several communities, perhaps containing just part of a village.

Domesday Book is available in facsimile (by the Ordnance Survey, 1861-4) and in translation in your *Victoria County History*. Domesday statements are not easy to understand without guidance. V. H. Galbraith in *The Making of Domesday Book* (1961) shows why and how the survey was compiled, interpreting many puzzling Domesday practices. H. C. Darby with others has published since 1952 a series of regional books on the Domesday geography of England.

Subsidies from clerics and laymen began in the thirteenth century. Taxpayers gave a proportion of their property, so surviving lists are useful in assessing local wealth and, with care, population. People are actually named in subsidies up to 1332 and in the complete lay subsidy of 1524-25. The poll taxes, too, of 1377-81 name people, but families are dodging the collector in 1381 producing what would seem a considerable fall in population. The subsidy of 1334 is useful for estimating township wealth while the 1428 parish tax, in excusing places with fewer than ten households, indicates backwardness and the process of village desertion. Latin numerals and names in these lists are not too difficult to decipher.

Householders paid a tax on each of their hearths during the late seventeenth century. A township officer compiled a list of all houses in his village, naming occupiers and noting the number of fireplaces. He divided people into two categories: taxpayers and paupers. In theory every house should appear, enabling the researcher to work out approximate population figures (say $4\frac{1}{2}$ persons per house). Check occupiers' names and see if these people left wills in the diocesan registry. Do wills describe the cottages? How many hearths went undeclared? Township returns survive in county records or in the muniments of a local landowner. The Public Record Office provides photocopies of hearth taxes between 1662 and 1674. The best year to choose is Lady Day 1664.

Chancery

The chancellor was originally king's chaplain. He became adviser on all aspects of government because of his learning, gradually organising a civil service. Records of this department survive from 1199 and mention most places in the country.

Chancery close rolls date from the thirteenth century to 1903. The rolls themselves contain copies of private letters, orders and other documents sent out by the king. On the back of the parchments are copies of documents such as house deeds, wills, conveyances of bankrupts' estates, charity papers, deeds of papists, surrenders of land (including monastic property), trust deeds of charity land including nonconformist chapels and village schools. These documents are indexed to some extent so it is worth looking under the name of your own town.

The royal secretarial office also heard law cases and petitions especially those that affected the king's person and rights very closely. Chancery proceedings date from 1386 to 1875. Evidence is often very detailed, recalling histories of persons and places back for two or three generations. Some records are well calendared. Make a start with the Record Commission's *Calendar of Proceedings in Chancery in the Reign of Elizabeth, with earlier examples* (1827-1832).

Inquisitions *post mortem* were taken by the Crown after the death of tenants in chief. These documents are estate surveys and valuations to determine death duties. They usually give a summary of family history and tell the name, age and relationship of the deceased's heirs. Inquisitions date from the thirteenth century until the Civil War period. Some are calendared and translated. For a guide to inquisitions see *Amateur Historian*, volume 6 number 7 (1965). Even more important for sidelights on family life and local customs are the inquisitions known as proofs of age.

Special commissions of Chancery date from the fourteenth century. One commission dealt with the decay of tillage through the enclosing of arable land for sheep pasture in the generation prior to 1517. Many returns are printed in Latin in I. S. Leadam *The Domesday of Inclosures* (1897).

Royal courts

The Royal Court at Westminster dealt with every problem of justice and administration. During the thirteenth century this Curia Regis divided into three courts of record: Common Pleas, Exchequer and King's Bench. Records of the Common Pleas date from 1182 to 1875. Judges also went round the country and held assize courts, and records include eyre (1206-1348) and assize (1248-1482) rolls. The royal justices have always dealt with most serious offences like theft, fraud and murder that affected the peace of the countryside. As a result court documents are usually very informative.

Early court records are in Latin but there are available some indexes, calendars and transcripts. Some are found in typescript only at the Public Record Office. These calendars will indicate village name, details of property in the case, parties to the suit and date.

State papers

Records of the various departments of state from Tudor times onwards deal with almost every village in the country. Lists and calendars cover some of the most useful series, especially state papers domestic, which relate the central government's intimate knowledge of local affairs.

Census returns

Census returns provide a complete list of inhabitants of every village and town in the land for 1841, 1851, 1861 and 1871. The first census was taken in 1801 but this return and subsequent ones of 1811, 1821 and 1831 show numbers of people and houses but no names. Of course these early documents are invaluable in providing the first reliable indication of local population. The 1831 census contains a breakdown of the numbers of men in the main fields of occupation: farming, trade, handicrafts, factories, mines, domestic service. But this classification is very dependent on the interpretation of the local census officer, and results have to be treated with care. These returns of 1801-31 are printed and are available in most libraries.

The returns of 1841-71 are handwritten on printed forms arranged by counties, parishes and townships. In each township all houses generally appear in street order sometimes with an address. Then all inhabitants are listed by name. Ages, jobs and birthplaces are detailed. The 1851-71 returns enable you to tell exactly when and where people were born. Returns after 1841 are preserved in the Public Record Office. Some libraries and county record offices possess microfilms of county returns. Microfilms or photocopies may be purchased by anyone.

Parliamentary papers

Parliamentary papers include records of the Lords and Commons and those published by command of the monarch. Each document is issued separately for sale, and at the conclusion of the session all papers are bound in volumes. It is these volumes – or microfiche copies – that are nowadays in public libraries. House of Commons sessional papers are divided into bills; reports of Commons committees; reports of royal commissioners; and accounts and papers. House of Lords documents follow a similar pattern. See W. R. Powell *Local History from Blue Books: a select list of the Sessional Papers of the House of Commons* (Historical Association, 1962). Papers nearly always contain evidence of witnesses in full with indexes of names and subjects. There are several good indexes including the reprint of *Hansard's Catalogue and Breviate of Parliamentary Papers 1696–1834* (1953) and P. & G. Ford *Select List of British Parliamentary Papers 1833–1899* (1953).

The printed sessional papers of the Lords contain little that is not in the Commons' papers. But the Lords have since 1497 amassed a great manuscript collection that has never been printed. Since 1603 there is a large file for every week of the session. Original papers are supplemented by committee books, evidence books, plans and so on dealing with such various topics as estates, dioceses, naturalisation, waterways and industry. Look especially at the protestation returns of 1642 naming all men over eighteen who signed or refused to sign the oath to maintain the reformed Protestant religion. Here is a true parochial census and an indication of division of opinion at the opening of the Civil War. Returns are listed in the appendix to the fifth report of the Historical Manuscripts Commission. The Lords records also contain one of England's most extensive collections for transport history.

Original documents of Lords and Commons are in the House of Lords Record Office. The Stationery Office has issued a calendar of Lords records (1497-1714).

Statutory authorities for special purposes

Turnpike trusts took over the maintenance of main roads when villages proved incapable of coping. Composed of landowners and merchants the trusts were established by parliament from 1663 until the coming of the railways to collect tolls at turnpike gates for the improvement of highways. For the history of roads between about 1710 and 1870 look for the turnpike act of parliament, the plan of the project in quarter sessions records, and the trust's own minutes, accounts, letters and plans. Records of the trusts may still lie with the solicitor whose predecessors served as clerks. Luckily many are in county archives.

Boards of guardians were set up under the 1834 Poor Law Amendment Act to administer poor relief. Already in the eighteenth century several groups of towns had joined together to build workhouses where able-bodied poor might work. But from 1834 the government compelled parishes to form unions with appointed officials and elected guardians of the poor to supplant parochial relief methods. All people needing relief – aged, impotent, vagabonds, children – were sent to a central workhouse. Records dating from 1834 to 1930 include minutes of guardians' meetings, accounts, lists of paupers, registers of births and deaths, health reports and detailed township rate books. Union records may be with the firm of solicitors that served as clerks to the guardians, at the workhouse or local district council office or with county archivists.

Local boards of health were set up in towns (not boroughs) after 1848 but were superseded by urban district councils in 1894. Minutes and letters relate to disease, sanitation and epidemics, extremely important topics for Victorian studies. Records may be with your local council or at the record office.

Highway boards covering parishes may have been set up locally between 1862 and 1894. Minutes, accounts and letterbooks deal with road maintenance in face of railway dominance. Documents are with the council or county record office.

CONCLUSION

Local history research is a continuing process. There is usually some other earthwork or recently discovered bundle of deeds to be examined. But if you have to end your work, perhaps to get the account into printer's hands, make sure that you have interpreted your material correctly and completely. Did Thomas Baker really hand over 5 messuages, 2 cottages, 200 acres arable, 300 acres pasture to William Brown? Was not this just a fictitious conclusion to a suit with wider and very significant implications for village development? You have described well enough the grassy ruins of the thirteenth-century manor-house and the more substantial derelict Victorian hall nearby. But why were these places abandoned? What was the effect on villagers' lives?

As you become expert in your local studies look again at the landscape, fields and buildings, ruins and factories. Consult once more all types of documentary material. You will be surprised how much detail you missed or misinterpreted at first glance. Among a mass of family and business records I sought for intimate glimpses of one family's life in the face of local industrialisation. I found maps and deeds and wills and physical remains galore, but no gossip or description. At the close of my research I went through the five thousand documents again. I'd already noticed several letters from cousins in Pennsylvania dated 1795-1812. Letters, I realised, demanded answers. Descendants of these cousins, now in far-away California, have indeed preserved letters from England, describing in great detail family scandals, hardships and joys in a growing and prosperous English factory town about 1800.

When you have examined all the obvious sources of local history, let the records point you to the less obvious and perhaps more significant source as well.

SOME RECORD REPOSITORIES IN BRITAIN

The following list is based on a handbook prepared by a joint committee of the Historical Manuscripts Commission and the British Records Association (fourth edition, HMSO 1971). By no means all local record offices are included below.

LONDON
There are at least one hundred repositories in London whose documents may be of interest. These include government, religious, banking and borough archives, records of national institutions like the railways, of city livery companies, of societies and colleges and of religious foundations. Only a selection is listed here. Consult the Greater London Record Office for detailed help.

Public Record Office, Chancery Lane, W.C.2.
Church Commissioners, 1 Millbank, S.W.1.
Duchy of Cornwall Office, 10 Buckingham Gate, S.W.1.
House of Lords Record Office, House of Lords, S.W.1.
Principal Probate Registry, Somerset House, Strand, W.C.2.
Department of Manuscripts, British Museum, W.C.1.
Lambeth Palace Library, S.E.1. (Canterbury Archdiocese records).
Methodist Archives and Research Centre, Epworth House, 25-35 City Road, E.C.1.
Society of Friends' Library, Friends' House, Euston Road, N.W.1.
Westminster Abbey Muniment Room and Library, The Cloisters, Westminster Abbey S.W.1.
British Railways Board, Historical Records Office, 66 Porchester Road, W.2.
Corporation of London Records Office, Guildhall, E.C.2.
Guildhall Library, Basinghall Street, E.C.2.
Greater London Record Office (London Records), County Hall, S.E.1.
Greater London Record Office (Middlesex Records), 1 Queen Anne's Gate Buildings, Dartmouth Street, S.W.1.
Corporation Muniment Room, Guildhall, Kingston-upon-Thames.
Southwark Diocesan Records and Lewisham Archives Department, The Manor House, Old Road, Lee, S.E.13.
College of Arms, Queen Victoria Street, E.C.4.
Society of Genealogists, 37 Harrington Gardens, S.W.7.
Registrar General, General Register Office, Somerset House, Strand, W.C.2.
Customs and Excise, Mark Lane, E.C.3.
Dr. Williams's Library, 14 Gordon Square, W.C.1. (nonconformist).
Westminster Public Libraries, Buckingham Palace Road, S.W.1. (Westminster parishes).

AVON Bristol Archives Office, Council House, Bristol 1.

BEDFORDSHIRE County Record Office, County Hall, Bedford.

BERKSHIRE County Record Office, Shire Hall, Reading.

BUCKINGHAMSHIRE County Record Office, County Offices, Aylesbury.
Buckinghamshire Archaeological Society, County Museum, Aylesbury.

CAMBRIDGESHIRE County Record Office, Shire Hall, Castle Hill, Cambridge.
University Library, Cambridge.
University Archives, Old Schools, Cambridge.

CHESHIRE County Record Office, The Castle, Chester.
City Record Office, Town Hall, Chester.
Public Library, Museum Street, Warrington.

CORNWALL County Record Office, County Hall, Truro.
Royal Institution of Cornwall, River Street, Truro.

CUMBRIA Cumberland, Westmorland, and Carlisle Record Office, The Castle, Carlisle, and County Hall, Kendal.
Public Library, Ramsden Square, Barrow-in-Furness.

DERBYSHIRE County Record Office, County Offices, Matlock.

DEVON County Record Office, County Hall, Exeter.
City Library, Castle Street, Exeter.
Cathedral Library, The Bishop's Palace, Exeter.

RECORD REPOSITORIES

DORSET County Record Office, County Hall, Dorchester.

DURHAM County Record Office, County Hall, Durham.
Palatinate, Capitular and Bishopric records, The Prior's Kitchen, The College, Durham

ESSEX County Record Office, County Hall, Chelmsford.

GLOUCESTERSHIRE County Records Office, Shire Hall, Gloucester.

GREATER MANCHESTER Central Library, St. Peter's Square, Manchester 2.
Chetham's Library, Manchester 3.
John Rylands Library, Deansgate, Manchester 3.
Local History and Archives Department, Central Library, Wigan.

HAMPSHIRE County Record Office, The Castle, Winchester.
City Record Office, Guildhall, Portsmouth.
Civic Record Office, Civic Centre, Southampton.
City Record Office, Guildhall, Winchester.
Cathedral Library, The Cathedral, Winchester.

HEREFORD AND WORCESTER County Record Office, The Old Barracks, Harold Street, Hereford.
County Record Office, Shire Hall, Worcester.

HERTFORDSHIRE County Record Office, County Hall, Hertford.

HUMBERSIDE County Record Office, County Hall, Beverley.
Registry of Deeds, Beverley.

ISLE OF WIGHT County Record Office, County Hall, Newport.

KENT Archives Office, County Hall, Maidstone.
Cathedral Library and City Record Office, The Precincts, Canterbury.
Diocesan Registry and Cathedral Library, c/o Messrs. Arnold, Tuff and Grimwade, The Precincts, Rochester.

LANCASHIRE County Record Office, Preston.

LEICESTERSHIRE County Record Office, 57 New Walk, Leicester.
City Record Office, Museum and Art Gallery, Leicester.

LINCOLNSHIRE County Archives Office, The Castle, Lincoln.
Gentlemen's Society, Spalding.

MERSEYSIDE City Record Office, Brown Library, Liverpool 3.

MIDDLESEX See under LONDON.

NORFOLK Norfolk and Norwich Record Office, Central Library, Norwich.

NORTH YORKSHIRE County Record Office, County Hall, Northallerton.
Registry of Deeds, Northallerton.
York Diocesan Records, Borthwick Institute of Historical Research, St. Anthony's Hall, York.
City Library, Museum Street, York.

NORTHAMPTONSHIRE County Record Office, Delapré Abbey, Northampton.

NORTHUMBERLAND County Record Office, Melton Park, North Gosforth, Newcastle upon Tyne 3.

NOTTINGHAMSHIRE County Records Office, County House, High Pavement, Nottingham.
Southwell Diocesan Registry, Church House, Park Row, Nottingham.

OXFORDSHIRE County Record Office, County Hall, New Road, Oxford.
Archdeaconries of Oxford and Berkshire and Oxford Diocesan Registry, Bodleian Library, Oxford.
University Archives, Bodleian Library, Oxford.

SALOP County Record Office, New Shirehall, Abbey Foregate, Shrewsbury.
Borough Archives, Guildhall, Shrewsbury.

SOMERSET County Record Office, Obridge Road, Taunton.

SOUTH YORKSHIRE West Riding archives and diocesan records, Archives Department, Central Library, Sheffield 1.

STAFFORDSHIRE County Record Office, County Buildings, Eastgate Street, Stafford.
in association with
Joint Record Office and Lichfield Diocesan Registry, Bird Street, Lichfield.
also in association with
William Salt Library, 19 Eastgate Street, Stafford.

SUFFOLK County Record Office, County Hall, Ipswich.
Bury St. Edmunds branch: 8 Angel Hill.

SURREY County Record Office, County Hall, Kingston-upon-Thames.
Museum and Muniment Room, Castle Arch, Guildford.

SUSSEX West Sussex Record Office, Wren House, West Street, Chichester.
East Sussex Record Office, Pelham House, Lewes.

TYNE AND WEAR City Archives Office, 7 Saville Place, Newcastle upon
Tyne 1.

WARWICKSHIRE County Record Office, Shire Hall, Warwick.
City Library, Ratcliff Place, Birmingham 1.
City Record Office, 9 Hay Lane, Coventry.
Borough Archives, Shakespeare's Birthplace Trust Library, Henley Street, Stratford-on-Avon.

WEST YORKSHIRE West Riding archives and diocesan records, Archives
Department, Sheepscar Branch Library, Leeds 7.
Brotherton Library, University of Leeds, Leeds 2.
Yorkshire Archaeological Society, Claremont, Clarendon Road, Leeds 2.
Registry of Deeds, County Hall, Wakefield.

WILTSHIRE County Record Office, County Hall, Trowbridge.
Diocesan Record Office, The Wren Hall, 56c The Close, Salisbury.

WALES National Library of Wales, Aberystwyth.
CLWYD County Record Office, The Old Rectory, Hawarden, Deeside.
DYFED County Record Office, County Hall, Carmarthen.
County Record Office, The Castle, Haverfordwest.
GWENT County Record Office, County Hall, Newport.
GWYNEDD County Record Office, Shire Hall, Llangefni.
County Record Office, County Offices, Dolgellau.
County Record Office, County Offices, Caernarvon.
SOUTH GLAMORGAN County Record Office, County Hall, Cathays Park, Cardiff.

SCOTLAND
Documents are kept by towns rather than by counties. The Scottish Record Office
is the most important centre for research.
Scottish Record Office, H.M. General Register House, Edinburgh 2.
National Library of Scotland, George IV Bridge, Edinburgh 1.
Office of Lord Lyon King of Arms, H. M. Register House, Edinburgh.
Scots Ancestry Research Council, North Saint David Street, Edinburgh.
City Archives, City Chambers, Edinburgh 1.
Registrar General's Office, New Register House, Edinburgh 2.
City Archives Office, City Chambers, Glasgow C.1.

NORTHERN IRELAND Public Record Office of Northern Ireland, Balmoral Avenue
Belfast.
Registrar General, Ormeau Avenue, Belfast 2.

EIRE Registrar General's Office, Custom House, Dublin.
Public Record Office of Ireland, Four Courts, Dublin.
Cheif Herald of Ireland, The Castle, Dublin.

INDEX

Accounts 43
Air photographs 7-8, 15
Apprenticeship 44
Archives 32, 33

Barrows 16-17
Bishop's records 46
Boundaries 13
Business records 53-5

Canals 30-1, 51, 52, 53
Card-index 5
Castles 9
Census returns 58
Chancery records 56-7
Charities 44
Church 17, 18
Church archives 45-50
Court records 42, 44, 57
Crosses 17-18
Custumals 43

Dating 34
Deserted sites 13
Diocesan records 46-7
Directories 8-9
Documents 32-4
Domesday Book 55-6

Electoral lists 52
Enclosures 16, 37-8
Engines 28-9
Estate papers 38-41
Exchequer records 55-6

Fields 15-16
Fieldwork 10-12
Fire insurance 54-5
Forests 20-1
Fortifications 18

Government records
  55-60
Graveyards 18
Guild records 45

Harleian Society 7

Houses 23-6

Illustrations 7
Industrial archaeology
  26-32
Inns 51
Iron production 30

Judicial records 50-1

Kip, Johannes 7

Land tax 52-3
Leases 39
Local government
  records 41-5

Machines 27-28, 29
Machines 27-8, 29
Magazines 8
Manorial and Tithe
  Documents Registers
  38
Manorial records 42-3
Maps 34-8
Markets 13
Marriage bonds 47-8
Methods of research 4-5
Mills 28
Mining 30
Minutes 43
Museums 9

National Buildings
  Record 7
National Register of
  Archives 38
Newspapers 8
Nonconformists 52
Notes of sources 4-5

Observation of land 9-10
Ordnance Survey 35

Palaeography 33
Parish records 49
Parks 21

Parliamentary papers
  58-9
Place-names 21-3
Plan of settlement 12-13
Poor law 51, 59
Power 28-9
Probate records 48

Quarter sessions 50-3

Railways 31-2, 51, 53
Rate books 43
Reading 5-6
Record office, county
  32-3, 61-3
Record Office, Public
  33, 42, 55
Records in print 6-7
Rentals 39
Research methods 4-5
Roads 19-20,51, 53, 59
Royal courts 57

Sale, notices of 41
School records 50
Settlement, place of
  43, 51
Settlement, reasons for
  10-12
Solicitors' accumulations
  54-5
State papers 57
Statutory authorities 59
Suburbs 14
Surveying a site 27

Tax records 44, 56
Textile industry 29
Tithe maps 36
Title deeds 39-41
Tombs 16-17
Town books 41-5
Town maps 36-7
Turnpikes 20, 59

Waterways 30-31
Wills 48

Printed by C. I. Thomas & Sons (Haverfordwest) Ltd.,
Press Buildings, Merlins Bridge, Haverfordwest, Pembs.